Mrs. Langley watched curiously as her daughter Anne finished dressing one morning. She pulled on her green pants and then turned the pockets inside out. Searching around in her drawer, Anne found an old blue sweater, turned the sleeves out and put it on backwards. Last, she took a rabbit's foot out of a little red box and slipped it around her neck.

"Where are you going dressed like that, Anne?"

"I'm off to school. We're having a math test today and then I have to recite a poem that I haven't even read yet. Mona told me that if I dressed this way, I would have good luck all day. And I'm going to need every bit I can get!"

THAT'S THE SILLIEST THING I'VE EVER SEEN!

1. **The main idea of this story is:**

   a. studying for a math test
   b. a girl who believes in good luck charms
   c. dressing up for school

2. **You might think Anne's behavior is somewhat**

   a. unusual.
   b. ordinary.
   c. proper.

3. **What kind of person is Anne?**

   a. a girl who studies hard
   b. a girl who believes in luck
   c. a girl who dresses well

4. **What phrase in the story means "to say from memory"?**

   a. to take a math test
   b. to recite something
   c. read from a book

5. **The story doesn't say, but Anne**

   a. probably had not studied her arithmetic.
   b. didn't know where her new sweater was.
   c. wanted to fool her mother.

Jeffrey likes to write letters in a secret way so that only his friends know what the message says. Summer vacation was coming to an end, and Jeff thought he had better call a meeting of the Purple Pack Rats Club. They needed to decide where they would go on their last hiking trip. Jeff closed the door to his room and wrote out the plan for each one of the boys. Can you work out the message?

1-A 2-B 3-C 4-D 5-E 6-F 7-G 8-H 9-I 10-J 11-K 12-L 13-M
14-N 15-O 16-P 17-Q 18-R 19-S 20-T 21-U 22-V 23-W 24-X
25-Y 26-Z

__ __ __ __ __ __ __   __ __ __ __ __ __ __ __
13 5   5   20 9   14 7   20 8   21 18 19 4   1   25

        __ __ __ __ __ :   __ __ __ __ __
        14 9   7   8   20   19 5   22 5   14

1. **The main idea of this story is:**

   a. writing secret messages to friends
   b. taking a vacation in September
   c. learning how to read and write

2. **Hiking can be a sport or a**

   a. race.
   b. hobby.
   c. dance.

3. **What month do you think it is?**

   a. November
   b. June
   c. August

4. **In the story "close" means "to shut". "Close" also means**

   a. far away.
   b. near to.
   c. things you wear.

5. **The story doesn't tell, but you might think Jeff**

   a. was President of the Purple Pack Rats.
   b. didn't want girls in the club.
   c. was younger than the other boys.

BE SURE TO EAT THE MESSAGE AFTER READING IT.

AGENT A-1

"What is this mess in my living room?" Mrs. Rogers shrieked. "Look at the walls, the rug, and Mr. Roger's favorite chair! Someone has a lot of explaining to do."

"Ernie invited us to his magic show," Betsey told Mrs. Rogers. "First he tried the tablecloth trick. He put some eggs, juice and sandwiches on the tablecloth and then with a wave of his hand, pulled it off. The trick didn't work. Everything was supposed to land on the table, but instead the food flew in every direction. We tried to clean it up, but the rug drank the milk. The windows were so hot today, the eggs just about fried the minute they hit the glass. One trick did work, though. Ernie made the canary disappear and now we can't find it."

WHERE COULD THAT BIRD HAVE GONE?

1. **The main idea of this story is:**

   a. a canary disappears
   b. Ernie gives an un-magic show
   c. frying eggs on the window

2. **"Mother shrieked at the sight." You might guess that**

   a. Mother was in the kitchen during the show.
   b. she was away from the house during the show.
   c. she was talking to Betsey during the show.

3. **What happened to the milk?**

   a. it soaked into the carpet
   b. it spilled on the chair
   c. it stayed in the glass

4. **Spell "flew" a different way and you will have**

   a. a word that means upset.
   b. a word that means ill.
   c. a word that means go away.

5. **How do you think mother feels about Ernie?**

   a. glad he has so much imagination
   b. angry because the canary has egg on it
   c. angry because the house is disorderly

"They're having a 'Most Beautiful Cat' contest in the park on Sunday and I'm going to enter Oliver," Sally told her big brother.

"That animal of yours is the poorest excuse for a cat that I have ever seen in my life! Oliver can't even purr very well," Phil laughed.

"Just you wait, Phil. When I get finished, Ollie will win a prize." Sally picked up the cat and went into her room. She mixed a few colors of her fingerpaints and then rubbed them into Oliver's fur, adding a few extra dots here and there. "What do you think now, Phil?"

Phil laughed so hard tears rolled down his face. "That's great, Sally. Only now you can't enter Oliver as a cat. He looks just like a ladybug with a tail."

1. **The main idea of the story is:**

    a. entering a cat in a contest
    b. a fingerpainting project
    c. a cat that doesn't purr

2. **Phil was sure that Oliver would not**

    a. win the contest.
    b. learn to purr.
    c. lose his fur.

3. **What doesn't the story tell?**

    a. how Phil felt about the cat
    b. what Sally put on Oliver's fur
    c. what kind of cat Oliver was

4. **"Poorest excuse for a cat" means**
    a. Oliver is not a very beautiful cat.
    b. Oliver looks just like a lady bug.
    c. Phil doesn't like cats.

5. **What colors do you think Sally painted Oliver?**

    a. black with green dots
    b. red with purple dots
    c. red with black dots

"Jonathan, will you please go to the store and get me some green beans, juice and ham? Hurry, I have to fix dinner soon."

On his way into town, Jonathan passed Mervin's Hobby Shop where a big green and yellow box in the window caught his eye. "That must be the new model Zip-A-Long Bi-Plane. I better go in just in case Mervin needs me to help him put it together."

Two hours passed before Jonathan realized he was supposed to be home by five. "Hm-m-m, where was I going before I got side-tracked? I'll go home and ask Mom. She'll know."

"You did it again, Jonathan? Every time you get near that hobby shop, your memory shuts off like a light switch. What will I do with you?"

1. **The main idea of this story is:**

   a. making a trip to the store
   b. a boy who gets side-tracked
   c. building a bi-plane

2. **Jonathan was not very good at**

   a. deciding what to buy.
   b. finding the store.
   c. remembering where he was going.

3. **When Jonathan went by the hobby shop he**

   a. bought some beans and ham.
   b. helped Mervin build a bi-plane.
   c. called his mother at home.

4. **A "way" can be a route to get to town. "Weigh" means:**

   a. thinned milk
   b. put something on a scale
   c. don't go too fast

5. **You might think Jonathan was**

   a. not very smart.
   b. a bad boy.
   c. sometimes forgetful.

"Our homework for tonight is to find out about our last names. How did we get the name 'Shields', Dad?"

"I don't know if this is exactly true, Nora, because the facts have never been written down, but I think this is the way the story goes. A very long time ago, one of my ancestors was a farmer in the hill country in England. His name was Henmonger which means he 'raised ducks and chickens'. He got tired of that work and moved to a village where he then made armor. Most people in those days took a last name that told about the kind of job they did. So, Mr. Henmonger changed his name to Mr. Shields because that is what he made - shields of armor. That's how we got our name."

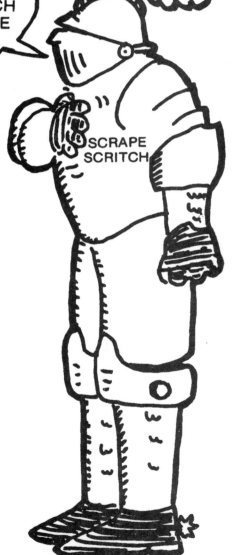

BOY, IT'S HARD TO SCRATCH AN ITCH THROUGH THESE THINGS!

SCRAPE SCRITCH

1. **The main idea of this story is:**

   a. What's in a name?
   b. how the Shields got their name
   c. a man who makes shields

2. **An ancestor is someone who was born**

   a. before you.
   b. after you.
   c. in July.

3. **Mr. Henmonger got his name from**

   a. a favorite chicken.
   b. the kind of job he did.
   c. the place where he lived.

4. **The word "raised" in this story means:**

   a. the chickens were lifted up high
   b. Mr. Shields breeds chickens on his farm
   c. chickens are fattened on grain

5. **From the story you might guess that**

   a. Mr. Shields kept his job making armor.
   b. raising chickens is not a good job.
   c. this story is not true.

On the day I was born, my uncle, grandfather, father, third cousin and another distant relative were at the hospital staring at me through the nursery window. "I think he looks just like me," Uncle Herman said. "You're mistaken, Herman," Cousin Ralph chimed in. "He's the image of his great-grandfather Melvin. No doubt about it!" Grandfather George got in the last word. "That boy's a Delancey for sure. Just look at that nose."

"I'll settle this," my father said calmly. "All of you wait here while I go down and sign the birth record."

And that is how I got my name: John Melvin Ralph George Herman Delancey Grant. Everyone calls me "J.G." for short.

1. **The main idea of this story is:**

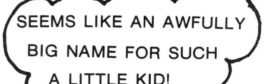

   a. how J.G. got his name
   b. visiting a new born baby
   c. birth records

2. **A relative is someone who is a member**

   a. of a private club.
   b. of your church.
   c. of your family.

3. **Which relative do you think is named John?**

   a. the grandfather
   b. the father
   c. the uncle

4. **"Record" here means certificate. Another "record" is**

   a. a return.
   b. an album.
   c. a direction.

5. **The story doesn't say, but you can guess that:**

   a. J.G. didn't like his long name.
   b. Father tried to please all the relatives.
   c. Grandfather didn't know Ralph very well.

7

Once a week, mostly on Fridays, our teacher gives us different kinds of puzzles to work out. Sometimes we have mind-benders and tongue-twisters, or crosswords and riddles, but my favorites are the jumbles. The teacher asks a question and then we unscramble the letters in the words to find the answer. I'm such a smart girl, I usually know the answer before I even work out the puzzle. One time, though, the teacher tried to fool me. Yesterday, this was the question we had to solve: "What is it that smells the worst?" Can you put the letters in order and find an answer?

HTIS ZULZPE AHS ON NSARWE

_____ _____ ____ ___ _____

1. **The main idea of this story is:**

   a. solving crosswords in class
   b. a puzzling jumble
   c. a good question for a puzzle

2. **Jumbles are puzzles where**

   a. words are upside down.
   b. letters are not in the right order.
   c. only eight letter words are used.

3. **When did the class work on puzzles?**

   a. whenever they wanted
   b. mostly on Mondays
   c. on the last school day of the week

4. **A "smell" is a**

   a. color.
   b. scent.
   c. cent.

5. **You might guess that the girl**

   a. didn't know how to unscramble words.
   b. never learned to read.
   c. knew a lot of riddles.

PUZZLE CHAMPION

CAREFUL! IT'S TRICKY!

Bucky Thornton drives me crazy sometimes. I never seem to be able to get a straight answer out of him. A simple "yes" or "no" to my questions would do most of the time. But Bucky can't resist including a silly saying or two in his answer. The other day I asked Bucky, "Why didn't Tony come to the baseball meeting yesterday?"

"Let me tell you what happened, James. Tony lost his glasses. He's as blind as a bat, you know, and probably couldn't find his way out of a paper bag without those glasses. After he fumbled around like an owl in daylight, Tony finally found his glasses just where he left them - on top of his head."

WHERE ARE THOSE GLASSES?

1. **The main idea of this story is:**

   a. a boy who can't give a straight answer
   b. getting ready for the baseball game
   c. a blind boy loses his glasses

2. **A silly saying could be:**

   a. dangerous
   b. humorous
   c. furious

3. **It is impossible for Bucky to give**

   a. an answer that is right.
   b. an answer that is to the point.
   c. an answer that is long.

4. **To "fumble like an owl in daylight" means:**

   a. Owls need glasses during the day.
   b. Owls probably don't see well in daylight.
   c. Owls cannot hunt very well.

5. **From the story, you cannot tell:**

   a. what Bucky said to James
   b. that Bucky uses silly sayings
   c. where the baseball meeting was held

When I was little, I used to think that if I grew up and became a dentist, I **would** never have to have my teeth drilled again. Or if I became a doctor, I **would** never be unhealthy another day in my life. Or maybe I would be a **teacher** and then I would never have to study anymore.

One day, my dentist pointed to his mouth and said, "See this tooth Doug? **It seems** the nerve died and now it will have to be drilled." If this could **happen** to a dentist, I figured a doctor could probably get sick, too. What **was** there left for me to be when I grew up?

I **guess** the only thing I would be is a grown-up. And the only thing I **would** not be is a little boy.

I KNOW! WHEN I GROW UP I'LL MAKE SOAP! THEN I'LL NEVER HAVE TO TAKE A BATH!

1. The main idea of this story is:

   a. that doctors never get sick
   b. growing up to be a grown-up
   c. dreaming about being a dentist

2. Doug thought doctors

   a. would be free of illness.
   b. gave diseases to other people.
   c. had their teeth drilled.

3. Why did Doug want to become a teacher?

   a. so he would know everything there is to know
   b. so he wouldn't have to be a plumber
   c. so he could work at night

4. Your mouth has 32 teeth. What else has teeth?

   a. a toothbrush
   b. a comb
   c. a newborn baby

5. Doug would probably think that policemen

   a. never went to jail.
   b. never got any sleep.
   c. never gave out tickets.

Janet felt great on this bright, sunny morning. "I don't even mind going to school. It's so pretty today." She whistled "Yankee Doodle Dandy" and skipped off down the street. At the corner of Wiley Street, Tommy Gray popped out from behind a gate:

" 'A whistling girl and crowing hen
Always come to no good end...'

My mom told me that little girls who whistle will grow a beard and my mother is always right! You better be careful, Janet!"

"Go away, Tommy. That doesn't really happen. It's just a silly superstition that someone made up a long time ago to scare girls."

1. **The main idea of this story is:**

   a. a boy who believes in superstitions
   b. Janet dancing on her way to school
   c. whistling girls grow beards

2. **Years ago, some superstitions developed**

   a. from months of hard work.
   b. to frighten people.
   c. from songs and dances.

3. **Tommy thought his mother**

   a. would like to meet Janet.
   b. didn't know much about girls.
   c. always told the truth.

4. **Which would be an example of a superstition?**

   a. a fear of going to school
   b. a lady in a full moon
   c. fear of Friday the 13th

5. **The story doesn't say, but Janet most likely**

   a. learned to sing instead of whistle.
   b. went right on whistling down the street.
   c. grew a beard the next day.

FS-32046 **Reading**

"Have a piece of cake, Mom, and a cookie too. I made them myself," said Lucy, passing the plate across the table. "I learned how to bake these in my science class. Our teacher has been demonstrating how we can better use natural foods in everything we eat."

"Ah-h-h! Lucy, what is this in my cookie? It doesn't look like a chocolate chip."

"It's an earthworm, Mother. Earthworms and insects are the foods of the future. Just think, you may never have to go to the grocery store again!"

1. **The main idea of this story is:**

   a. making earthworm cakes and cookies
   b. planning classes for the future
   c. some new foods in our future

2. **Another natural food might be:**

   a. a candy bar
   b. a beetle
   c. a root beer

3. **Mother probably didn't like**

   a. chocolate chip cookies.
   b. Lucy's English teacher.
   c. the taste of the cookies.

4. **The opposite of a natural food would be a**

   a. canned food.
   b. man-made food.
   c. sun-grown food.

5. **Many years ago, people ate insects because:**

   a. they did not know how to make bread
   b. they needed to get rid of them
   c. they were a healthy food

"You have a lot of ability, Arthur. I hope you will always take good care of it. Use it wisely and it will grow along with you."

Arthur wasn't really sure what the teacher meant, but he decided to take her advice and be extra careful with his ability. So he took it home and put it in the closet. "It'll be safe in here for a long time."

The years passed. One day, Arthur had to take an important test for a summer job. "I'll go home and get my ability and be right back," he told the man. But his ability wasn't in the closet anymore. "Oh, no! I've never used my ability all this time and now it's gone. I should have known I needed to use it every day so it would develop with me!"

GET IN THERE!

1. **The main idea of this story is:**

   a. hiding ability in the closet
   b. the ability that never grew
   c. Arthur loses a summer job

2. **A person's ability is usually a special**

   a. skill.
   b. operation.
   c. teacher.

3. **Why did Arthur put his ability in the closet?**

   a. because that is where it belongs
   b. because his teacher told him
   c. for safekeeping

4. **A "wise" person would be someone who**

   a. belongs in jail.
   b. tries hard.
   c. is simple.

5. **From the story, you can tell that Arthur did not**

   a. know how to take a test.
   b. understand what the teacher was saying.
   c. want to develop his ability.

  FS-32046 **Reading**

"I sure am getting tired of everyone walking in here every morning and gritting their teeth right in my face," the mirror reflected.

"Me, too," gurgled the faucet. "Look at this mess in my sink. It doesn't drain like it used to when it was young. All that toothpaste and shaving cream has clogged the pipes."

"I have the answer, Sir Faucet. Tomorrow morning, put a lock on your 'Cold'. If only hot water rushes out, steam will billow up and cover me with fog. No one brushes their teeth with hot water. This will be a triumph for mirrors and faucets everywhere!"

1. **The main idea of this story is:**

    a. a mirror and faucet plot a plan
    b. turning on the hot water
    c. shaving in a mirror

2. **The sink had probably been in the bathroom**

    a. just a few weeks.
    b. several years.
    c. since day before yesterday.

3. **What caused the pipes to clog?**

    a. thick toothpaste
    b. dirty water
    c. a bar of soap

4. **To "grit" your teeth means to**

    a. brush them up and down.
    b. grind them around.
    c. click them together.

5. **On line 4, who does the word "it" refer to?**

    a. the sink
    b. the faucet
    c. the pipes

"You could be a very good writer someday, Lisa," Mrs. Roberts told her. "But you need to learn to use more adjectives to describe your characters. Today, write me a story about what you would like to do this summer." A little later Lisa returned her paragraph to the teacher, and this is what she wrote:

> I want to go to camp again this summer. Last summer I rode a horse named "Happy New Year". He was the color of a cloudy sky with splashes of milk and he could run like lightning. I learned how to handle him so well, that after a few weeks I didn't need a saddle anymore. Someday I would like to work at that camp.

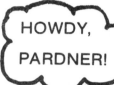

HOWDY, PARDNER!

1. The main idea of this story is:

a. telling about a summer job
b. using adjectives for an interesting story
c. practice in writing paragraphs for class

2. The name of the horse suggests he was born

a. at noon on a day in December.
b. on the first day of the year.
c. on no special day.

3. How did Lisa ride her horse?

a. side-saddle
b. without reins
c. bareback

4. To "run like lightning" means to

a. run during a rainstorm.
b. run very fast.
c. run over rooftops.

5. From the clues you can tell the horse's color was

a. gray with white spots.
b. cloudy and gray.
c. gray with milk splashed on.

Hermit Crabs

Lobsters, crabs, shrimps and barnacles are crustaceans. A crustacean is an animal with a crust. Most crustaceans have at least ten legs and four feelers. They live in water and breathe with gills as fish do.

Although a hermit crab is a crab, it looks more like a small lobster. The hind part of a hermit crab is not protected by a strong crusty shell, so it must use the shell of a sea snail to cover its soft parts. The kind of shell it uses depends on where it lives and upon its size. As the crab grows each shelter becomes too tight and it must search for a larger one. The hermit anchors itself inside its new home by means of its rear pair of tiny hooklike legs. The large pair of front legs has claws with which the hermit catches food— tiny fish and dead animal matter. These front claws also form a closed front door when it has gone completely inside the shell. Hermit crabs often have partners who live on their shell and act as camouflage. A sea anemone often looks like a beautiful flower growing on a shell. It enjoys eating scraps from the hermit crab's meals.

1. **This story is mainly about:**
   a. ocean creatures
   b. mammals in the sea
   c. shell-dwelling crabs

2. **When the hermit crab is without a shell:**
   a. it is unprotected
   b. it enjoys swimming
   c. it is safe from danger

3. **Hind legs of the hermit crab:**
   a. catch food
   b. hold it in the shell
   c. are used for protection

4. **What word means "to hold in place"?**
   a. cover
   b. anchor
   c. camouflage

5. **You can tell that hermit crabs:**
   a. have large, powerful hind legs
   b. must come to the surface to breathe
   c. have many homes in a lifetime

Polar Bears

Polar bears are smaller than you are at birth. They weigh one pound and are ten inches long. When full grown, polar bears can weigh seven hundred pounds. Newborn bears are helpless. In winter the female bear goes into a cave in an iceberg where she gives birth to one or two cubs. In springtime they leave the ice cave. Their white fur blends in with the Arctic ice and snow. Oil in their fur keeps them warm and dry. Fur on the bottom of their feet stops them from slipping on the ice. The polar bear has a different shape than most other bears. His head is smaller, his neck longer and his body more slender. This body shape helps make the Polar bear an excellent swimmer. They have been sighted in the ocean hundreds of miles from shore.

Polar bears eat plants, berries, seals, walruses and fish. Cubs learn to hunt and swim. They must learn everything they need to know in two years. The mother bear chases the cubs away when they reach two years of age. They must learn to survive on their own.

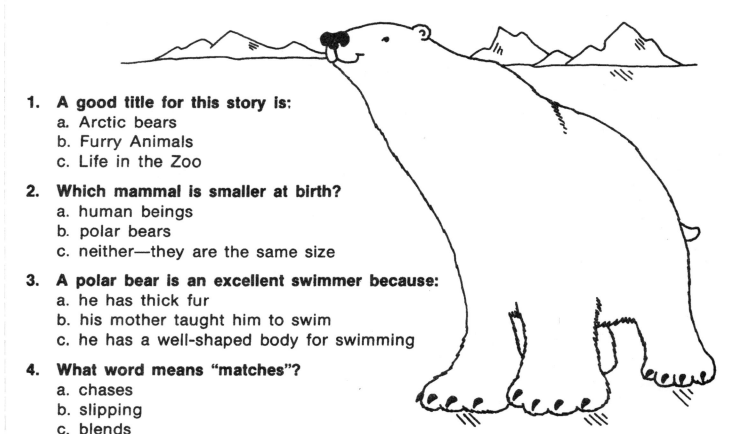

1. **A good title for this story is:**
   a. Arctic bears
   b. Furry Animals
   c. Life in the Zoo

2. **Which mammal is smaller at birth?**
   a. human beings
   b. polar bears
   c. neither—they are the same size

3. **A polar bear is an excellent swimmer because:**
   a. he has thick fur
   b. his mother taught him to swim
   c. he has a well-shaped body for swimming

4. **What word means "matches"?**
   a. chases
   b. slipping
   c. blends

5. **How do you think the bear cubs feel when their mother drives them away?**
   a. frightened
   b. happy
   c. sleepy

Turtles

Each kind of turtle has a different looking shell, but all turtles have shells. Turtles are born with a soft covering of shell and bone. As the turtle grows its shell hardens and grows too. The shell offers protection from enemies.

A map turtle has a wide, flat shell with bumpy edges. A soft-shelled turtle's shell looks like a green pancake. A box turtle has a high, round shell that can close up like a box. But if the box turtle eats too much it gets too big for its shell and its fat legs keep popping out. However, most turtles can grow to weigh over two hundred pounds.

Sea turtles spend all of their lives in water with one exception. They must come up on beaches to lay their eggs in a dry place high above the water. The female may lay as many as one hundred eggs that look much like a pile of ping pong balls before she covers them with sand.

1. **This story is mainly about:**
   a. how turtles are different
   b. how turtles protect themselves
   c. where turtles lay eggs

2. **If a box turtle eats too much:**
   a. he outgrows his shell
   b. he grows a larger shell
   c. his shell becomes soft

3. **Where does the sea turtle lay eggs?**
   a. shallow water
   b. tidepools
   c. dry beach

4. **Which word in the story means "gives"?**
   a. covering
   b. offers
   c. popping

5. **From reading the story you can tell that:**
   a. turtles cannot protect themselves
   b. turtles can weigh up to fifty pounds
   c. turtles can be identified by their shells

Orangutans

The orangutan sleeps high in a tree. His bed is made of leafy branches. He holds on tightly with his fingers and toes while sleeping. The five foot tall, one hundred pound animal has red, stringy hair. Orangutans are primates just like you. Monkeys, apes and man are in the primate group of animals. Orangutans spend most of their time in trees swinging from branch to branch. Their long arms help them swing through the trees searching for bird's eggs, bark, leaves and fruit to eat.

Orangutans are frequently seen in zoos. They live rather well in captivity, if they have the right food and proper care. The orangutan is considered to be an endangered animal. Too many have been caught and sold. Now they are protected by law and may not be captured anymore.

1. **This story is mostly about:**
   a. life in the jungle
   b. hunting for animals
   c. a tree-dwelling primate

2. **Orangutans are usually:**
   a. in trees
   b. sleeping
   c. walking on the ground

3. **In zoos orangutans need:**
   a. good food and care
   b. plenty of sleep
   c. sleep and exercise

4. **What word means "often"?**
   a. considered
   b. just
   c. frequently

5. **You can tell that:**
   a. orangutans can't live in zoos
   b. orangutans could all be killed if not protected by law
   c. orangutans hunt animals for food

     FS-32046 Reading

Dogs

The dog has been man's best friend for thousands of years. They are usually friendly and learn to mind well. All over the world, dogs are trained to help people in work and play. They are ranked fifth in intelligence and were the first animal to be tamed by man. They make good guards and can protect people and their possessions. Sometimes dogs are used to help policemen in their work. Specially trained dogs lead blind persons. Dogs like to be with people and are especially happy when they are with children.

A puppy should be house-trained as soon as it is taken from its mother. He must learn to follow directions. First he should be taught how to walk when wearing a leash. Then the puppy should be taught to come when his master calls. Dogs can be taught to follow many commands. A dog should be rewarded with kind words and pats when he does something right.

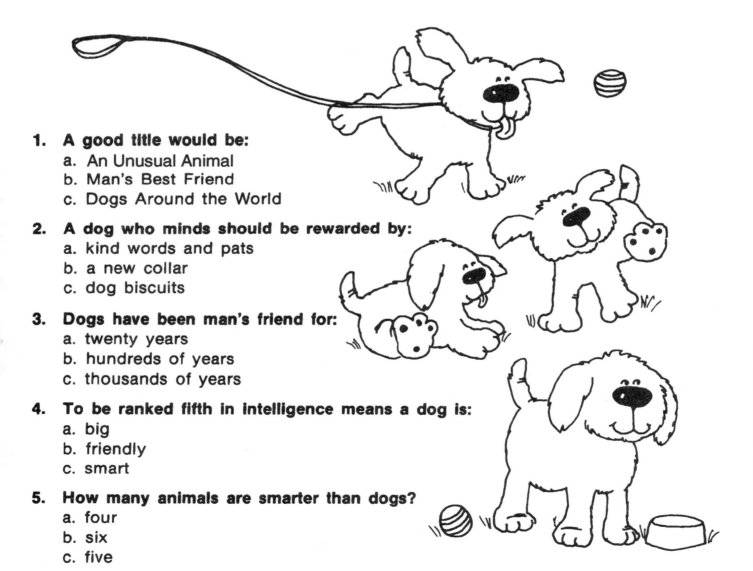

1. **A good title would be:**
   a. An Unusual Animal
   b. Man's Best Friend
   c. Dogs Around the World

2. **A dog who minds should be rewarded by:**
   a. kind words and pats
   b. a new collar
   c. dog biscuits

3. **Dogs have been man's friend for:**
   a. twenty years
   b. hundreds of years
   c. thousands of years

4. **To be ranked fifth in intelligence means a dog is:**
   a. big
   b. friendly
   c. smart

5. **How many animals are smarter than dogs?**
   a. four
   b. six
   c. five

Bats

Bats are the only flying mammals. The small mouse-like animals have long, thin fingers. Thin skin that spreads between the fingers forms the wings. There are over two thousand kinds of bats. Some people are afraid of bats. They think bats will fly into them. This is not true because bats can "see" in total darkness. They can't see with their eyes so they make sounds as they fly. These sounds are too high for us to hear. The sounds echo and the bat can tell when it is coming close to something. Hundreds of bats can fly in a dark cave without ever crashing into the walls or into one another.

Hind claws help the bat hang upside down for sleeping. Most bats are nocturnal animals so they sleep during the day and hunt for food at night. They fly through the darkness scooping up insects by the hundreds. Bats help man by eating insect pests.

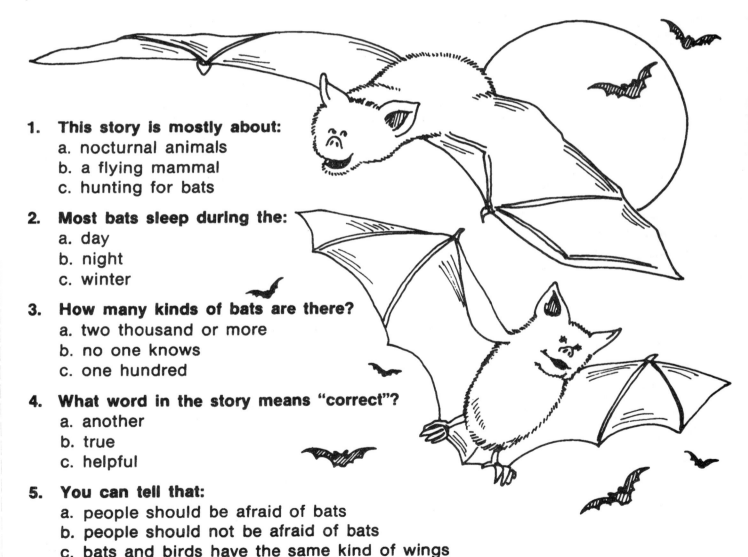

1. **This story is mostly about:**
   a. nocturnal animals
   b. a flying mammal
   c. hunting for bats

2. **Most bats sleep during the:**
   a. day
   b. night
   c. winter

3. **How many kinds of bats are there?**
   a. two thousand or more
   b. no one knows
   c. one hundred

4. **What word in the story means "correct"?**
   a. another
   b. true
   c. helpful

5. **You can tell that:**
   a. people should be afraid of bats
   b. people should not be afraid of bats
   c. bats and birds have the same kind of wings

 FS-32046 Reading

Dolphins

The dolphin is one of the fastest swimmers in the sea. Their powerful tails beat up and down when they swim. The tail and flippers are used for steering. Their mouths are curved to look like a big, happy grin. These friendly mammals are related to whales and porpoises. Dolphins can stay under water for four to six minutes. While sleeping they come to the surface to breathe without waking up. Breathing is done through a blowhole on top of the dolphin's head. The Bottlenose dolphins are seven to eleven feet long and weigh three to seven hundred pounds.

Baby dolphins are born tail first under the water. Other dolphins gather around to help. They help the baby go up to the surface for air and guard it against sharks. A young dolphin stays with its mother until it is about eighteen months old.

A dolphin's language is made up of clicks, whistles and grunts. These sounds echo back to tell them where to find food. They see with their ears, as bats do. Man has not yet learned to understand dolphin language. Dolphins like to be with humans and have been trained to help people.

1. **This story is mostly about:**
   a. how dolphins live
   b. life in the sea
   c. air breathing fish

2. **Dolphins can remain underwater for:**
   a. twenty minutes
   b. two minutes
   c. four to six minutes

3. **Dolphin language:**
   a. is understood by man
   b. has never been heard by man
   c. is not yet understood by man

4. **Which word in the story means "strong"?**
   a. powerful
   b. guard
   c. understand

5. **You can tell that:**
   a. dolphins are afraid of people
   b. dolphins fight with one another
   c. dolphins are intelligent animals

Cats

Fierce lions and tigers are like your pet cat in many ways. All cats belong to the same cat family. Helpless newborns are blind and must be cared for by the mother cat. Cats have a rough tongue that cleans their fur. The mother washes the kittens until they are big enough to keep themselves clean. She watches over them until they are old enough to hunt for food. All cats are meat-eaters. They have an instinct for hunting.

Cats have round heads and small noses. Their strong legs help them to run and jump. All cats have five toes on their front paws and four on the hind paws. Each toe has a sharp, curved claw. Padded feet allow the cat to move quietly. The cheetah is a member of the cat family. In a burst of speed it can run seventy miles per hour! The cheetah is the world's fastest running animal.

Cats' eyes change according to the light. When it is dark their pupils open wide to let them see in the dark. Cats can see quite well in the dark. Most cats hunt for food at night.

1. **This story is mostly about:**
   a. the cat family
   b. how cats hunt for food
   c. newborn cats

2. **Strong legs, padded feet and claws:**
   a. are not important to cats
   b. are only found on lions and tigers
   c. help all cats hunt for meat

3. **On their front paws cats have:**
   a. four toes
   b. five toes
   c. three toes

4. **Which word in the story means "not smooth"?**
   a. fierce
   b. padded
   c. rough

5. **Your pet cat is:**
   a. exactly like a cheetah
   b. in the same family as lions and tigers
   c. not a meat-eater

23

Skunks

Skunks are known for their strong, unpleasant odor. The skunk uses his scent to protect itself from enemies. An animal sprayed by a skunk will smell awful for days. Before spraying, the skunk warns that he is frightened by stamping his feet, clicking his teeth and hissing. It raises its tail to spray. The spray can reach thirteen feet, and the skunk usually hits whatever he wants to spray. The spray is not harmful, but it smells awful, makes your eyes burn and cannot be washed off.

Skunks live in burrows or hollow logs. They are nocturnal animals who roam around at night to find food. Skunks will eat almost anything. They turn over rocks and sniff around to find insects, nuts, fruit and reptiles. In the cold winter, skunks eat very little and sleep for several days at a time. They find a mate, and baby skunks are born in the spring.

The striped skunk is about the size of a large cat. It has a pointed nose and an arched back. Its thick, shiny black fur has two white stripes down the back. The skunk has short legs and walks as though its shoes are too tight. Skunks are easy to identify because of their coloring. If you see a skunk, do not get too close—you might get sprayed!

1. **The best name for this story is:**
   a. How to Catch a Skunk
   b. Where Skunks Live
   c. All About Skunks

2. **Skunks live in the:**
   a. woods
   b. desert
   c. tops of trees

3. **The skunk:**
   a. sprays without any warning
   b. stamps, clicks his teeth and hisses
   c. runs away when frightened

4. **What word in the story means "lifts"?**
   a. warns
   b. raises
   c. sprays

5. **You can tell that the skunk:**
   a. makes a good pet
   b. looks like a cat
   c. can protect itself

       FS-32046 Reading

Dinosaurs

Tyrannosaurus Rex (tie-ron-oh-sawr-us rex) was the most fierce animal that ever walked on the earth. It was eighteen to twenty feet tall and walked on its powerful hind legs. Its jaws were four feet long and contained long, sharp teeth. Its teeth and strong jaws were used for biting and tearing apart meat. This gigantic, meat-eating dinosaur killed animals, ate them and then slept for several days. Other dinosaurs were afraid of it.

We know dinosaurs lived long ago but no man has ever seen one. Dinosaurs lived millions of years before people appeared on earth. Fossils have told us the story of the dinosaurs. Fossils are the hardened remains of animals that lived many years ago. Scientists study fossils for information about the past. They found out how dinosaurs looked and what the land was like in dinosaur times. Bones of the Tyrannosaurous Rex were found in the state of Montana. Millions of years ago, when dinosaurs lived there, it was a warm, swampy jungle. Much of what is now the United States was covered by ocean water.

Scientists have not figured out why dinosaurs disappeared. Perhaps the jungles got colder and the dinosaurs could not live in cold weather. Some scientists believe small, furry animals ate dinosaur eggs so baby dinosaurs did not hatch and grow. Perhaps there was not enough food for the giant animals. Dinosaur skeletons can be seen in many museums.

1. **This story is mostly about:**
   a. dinosaur eggs
   b. animals who lived before man
   c. cave man and the dinosaurs

2. **Millions of years ago the land was:**
   a. colder
   b. warmer
   c. about the same as now

3. **We know about dinosaurs from:**
   a. museums
   b. old photographs
   c. fossils

4. **The word "disappeared" in the story means:**
   a. passed from sight
   b. figured
   c. no longer alive

5. **You can tell that dinosaurs:**
   a. hatched from eggs
   b. were playful
   c. can live in any climate

FS-32046 Reading

Toads

Toads spend the cold winter buried underground. They come out of hibernation in the warm springtime. Toads and frogs look much alike. Frogs have smooth skin and toads have rough, bumpy skin. Some people think you can get warts from touching toads, but that is not true.

Toads eat live insects. They will only eat things that move. Many kinds of toads have long, sticky tongues. The toad suddenly shoots out his tongue and the insect is caught. It cannot get away because it is stuck to the toad's tongue.

Toads gulp in air and force it into a sac in their throats. The toad makes a singing sound as it lets the air out. This song is a signal that it is breeding time. Toad eggs are lain in shallow water. Many are eaten by other animals. The rest hatch into tadpoles. Three months later the tadpole has changed into an air-breathing toad. Animals who are born to breathe underwater and later grow into air-breathing animals are called amphibians.

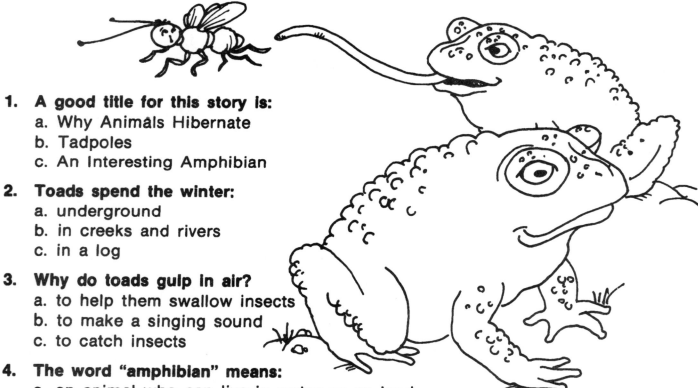

1. **A good title for this story is:**
   a. Why Animals Hibernate
   b. Tadpoles
   c. An Interesting Amphibian

2. **Toads spend the winter:**
   a. underground
   b. in creeks and rivers
   c. in a log

3. **Why do toads gulp in air?**
   a. to help them swallow insects
   b. to make a singing sound
   c. to catch insects

4. **The word "amphibian" means:**
   a. an animal who can live in water or on land
   b. an animal that remains underwater
   c. an animal that breathes underwater at birth but changes to an air-breather

5. **If you caught a toad you would probably:**
   a. get warts
   b. need a warm, dry home for it
   c. have trouble catching enough live insects for it

Fireflies

A firefly is an unusual insect. It has a yellow light that flashes on and off on the back part of its body. The firefly is about an inch long. It can be found in warm, grassy places in the summer. At night you can see their small lights blinking on and off. The male firefly blinks his light first. When he does this he is signaling to a female firefly that he is looking for a mate. If a female is nearby she will signal back by flashing her light. The lights are used to help the male and female fireflies get together.

Scientists know the light is used to bring the male and female firefly together. They do not understand exactly how the tiny insect makes its own light. The light is similar to a flashlight. There is a reflector behind the light and a clear place in front of it. The light goes on and is reflected out through the clear area on its body. People enjoy watching fireflies on warm summer nights.

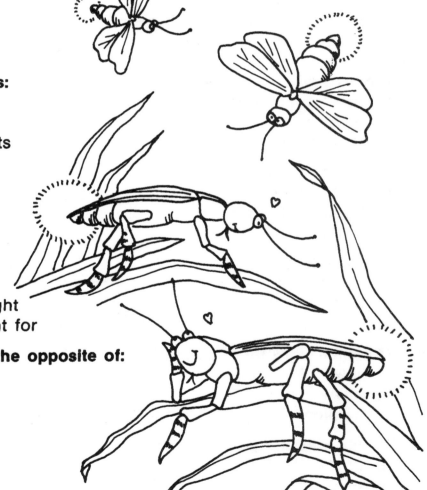

1. A good name for this story is:
   a. Insect Pests
   b. How to Catch Fireflies
   c. Insects with Flashing Lights

2. When do fireflies mate?
   a. on warm summer nights
   b. during hibernation
   c. during the day

3. Scientists don't know:
   a. how a flashlight works
   b. how fireflies make their light
   c. what fireflies use their light for

4. The word "together" means the opposite of:
   a. nearby
   b. apart
   c. friendly

5. Fireflies use their lights to:
   a. frighten other insects
   b. communicate
   c. make them fly faster

Porcupines

Can porcupines throw their quills? No, they cannot, but the quills do come out easily. The body of the porcupine is covered by quills that are several inches long. Each quill has a barb on the end like a fishhook. When a quill gets stuck in another animal it is very painful.

Rats, squirrels and porcupines are in the rodent family. They have big front teeth and will gnaw on almost anything. They love to gnaw on things that are salty. When people touch things they leave a tiny bit of salty perspiration. The porcupine gnaws on old shoes, tools or whatever he can find that people have touched. They eat fruit, vegetables, flowers and twigs, but never other animals. At times porcupines are troublesome pests. They gnaw on the bark of trees in the woods where they live. This causes many trees to die.

American porcupines are slow and clumsy on the ground. They are fast swimmers and good climbers.

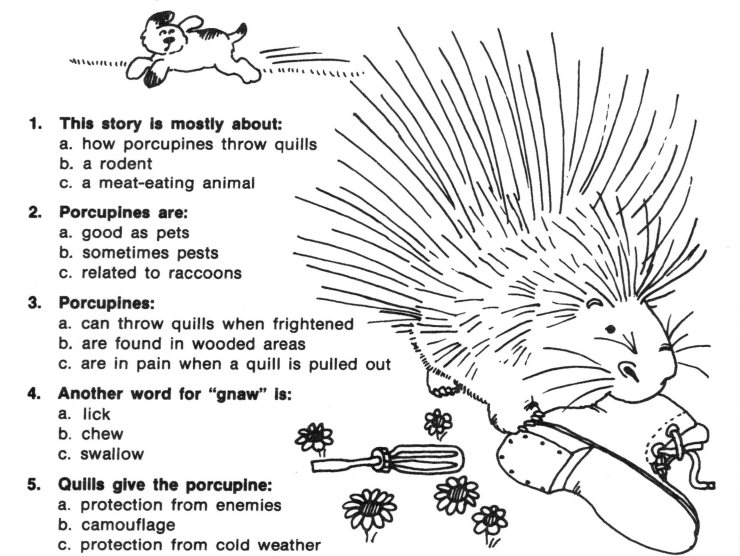

1. **This story is mostly about:**
   a. how porcupines throw quills
   b. a rodent
   c. a meat-eating animal

2. **Porcupines are:**
   a. good as pets
   b. sometimes pests
   c. related to raccoons

3. **Porcupines:**
   a. can throw quills when frightened
   b. are found in wooded areas
   c. are in pain when a quill is pulled out

4. **Another word for "gnaw" is:**
   a. lick
   b. chew
   c. swallow

5. **Quills give the porcupine:**
   a. protection from enemies
   b. camouflage
   c. protection from cold weather

FS-32046 Reading

Raccoons

Raccoons are easy to identify. They have five to seven rings of black fur around their bushy tails. Black fur is also around the raccoon's eyes in the shape of a mask. These nocturnal animals hunt in the dark for food.

Raccoons hiss, snarl and growl when they are angry. When they grunt and make a shrill sound they are happy. They can be fierce fighters. Long claws, forty teeth and strong jaws help the raccoon defend itself. Raccoons have five long fingers on their front paws. They can open latches, turn doorknobs and twist bottle caps. They are intelligent, curious animals who like to poke into things.

Birds, tadpoles, fish, fruit and vegetables are eaten by raccoons. They slosh their food around in water before eating it. Scientists do not think that raccoons are washing their food to clean it. They believe that raccoons wet their food for another reason, but they do not know exactly why. Some scientists believe raccoons can swallow wet food easier. Others think that raccoons learned to slosh food in water because they often find food in water. Maybe they do it just for fun!

1. **The best title for this story is:**
   a. The Raccoon—A Curious Animal
   b. Animals who Live in Trees
   c. Caring for a Pet Raccoon

2. **Raccoons can:**
   a. not swim
   b. open all sorts of things
   c. not see at night

3. **Scientists:**
   a. know raccoons will only eat clean food
   b. have never studied raccoons
   c. are not sure why raccoons wet their food

4. **"Intelligent" means:**
   a. careful
   b. curious
   c. smart

5. **Raccoons are:**
   a. intelligent and curious
   b. safe in their homes at night
   c. afraid of eating dirty food

 FS-32046 Reading

Rattlesnakes

Rattlesnakes are found in almost every state in the United States. The largest, most dangerous rattlesnake is the diamondback. It grows to be five to six feet long. Snakes are cold-blooded. They are warm when they are in a warm place and cold when they are in a cold place. Snakes often sun themselves on a warm rock to warm their bodies after a cool night. In winter snakes hibernate so they do not freeze to death.

All rattlesnakes have heads shaped like a triangle. They shed their skins as they grow bigger, and they continue to shed when full grown. They rub their heads on something rough to make a hole in the old skin. The skin peels back as they slowly wiggle out of the old skin. You may find a snakeskin in a field or in the woods some day. Snakes have no ears. Rattlesnakes catch food by using their eyes and pits. Pits are special holes that can sense when there is a warm animal nearby. There is a pit by each eye. Rattlesnakes eat mice, rats, rabbits and other small animals. They bite their prey and the animal dies in a few minutes. Long upper teeth called fangs are hollow so venom can flow through to the animal. When in danger rattlesnakes shake their tails. The rattle sound is a fast, clicking noise made by the bony rings on the rattlesnake's tail. This is a signal that a rattlesnake is frightened and may strike!

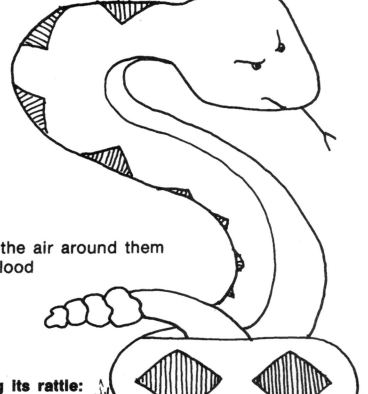

1. **This story is mostly about:**
   a. rattlesnakes
   b. all kinds of snakes
   c. food for snakes

2. **Rattlesnakes:**
   a. cannot be tamed
   b. are not often seen in winter
   c. squeeze their prey

3. **Cold-blooded animals:**
   a. are always cold
   b. are the same temperature as the air around them
   c. have warm bodies and cold blood

4. **The opposite of "dangerous" is:**
   a. harmful
   b. fierce
   c. harmless

5. **If you hear a rattlesnake shaking its rattle:**
   a. it is a warning
   b. it is hungry
   c. it is moving away

         FS-32046 Reading

Sea Horses

The sea horse is actually a fish but it doesn't act like one. There are twenty-five different kinds of sea horses. The largest kind grows to be twelve inches. Most sea horses are three to six inches long. They have two skeletons—one on the outside of their bodies and the other on the inside. Hard plates cover the sea horse like a suit of armor. Sea horses are usually gray or black.

The sea horse uses his tail much like a monkey does. The tail is wrapped around plants or coral to anchor it in place. Sea horses often hide in the same place for hours. When a sea horse wants to go forward or backward it moves its dorsal fin. The dorsal fin is in the middle of its back. Small animals are sucked into the sea horse's snout-shaped mouth for food.

Male sea horses have a pouch like a kangaroo. This pouch is part of the interesting way sea horses breed and care for their young. Eggs are put in the male's pouch by the female. The father sea horse gets very heavy and can hardly swim from the weight of the babies in his pouch. The babies grow inside the pouch for forty-five days. Then almost two hundred baby sea horses wriggle out of the pouch and swim away. Babies are not taken care of by their parents. They swim away to sea plants and hang on with their tiny tails. Many are eaten by ocean creatures. At five months they are fully grown.

1. **This story is mostly about:**
   a. horses
   b. an unusual fish
   c. aquarium life

2. **If you touched a sea horse it would feel:**
   a. hard
   b. very hot
   c. like a goldfish

3. **The sea horse:**
   a. swims by wiggling his body
   b. uses his tail to hang onto things
   c. has three skeletons

4. **"Anchor" means:**
   a. a ship
   b. to hold in place
   c. hard plates

5. **You can tell that:**
   a. sea horses are fully grown after a year
   b. sea horses take good care of their babies
   c. sea horses must quickly learn to take care of themselves

Guinea Pigs

Guinea pigs are rodents. They are not related to pigs. Why they are called Guinea pigs is a mystery. Guinea pigs come in a variety of colors. Their hair can be short, long, curly or straight. Guinea pigs are born with their eyes open and with a full coat of fur. They look like miniature adult guinea pigs. They love to eat and play at night and spend the days sleeping.

A pet guinea pig will need a cage. You can buy cages of wire or plastic. Cardboard boxes will not work because the animal can gnaw its way out. Like most rodents, guinea pigs like to gnaw. Give them some clothespins, twigs or a piece of hard wood to chew on. Gnawing files down their teeth which are always growing. Without gnawing the teeth would get too long. You can buy guinea pig food at the pet store. They also like bits of fruit and vegetables.

A cardboard box can be put in the cage. The guinea pig will have a grand time climbing in and out of the box. They are fun to watch.

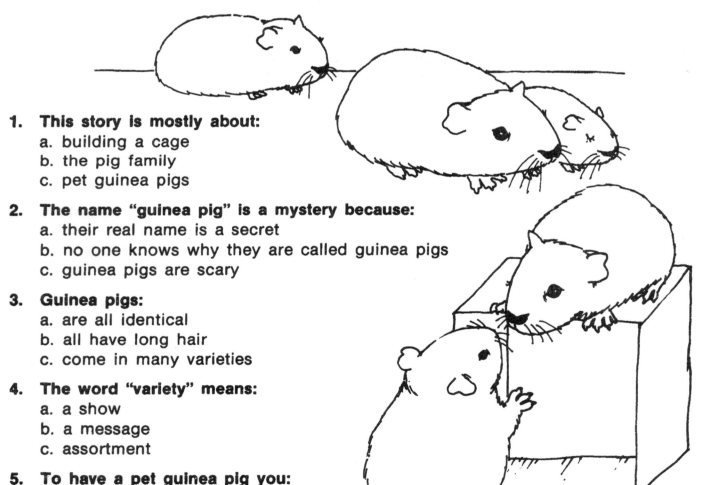

1. **This story is mostly about:**
   a. building a cage
   b. the pig family
   c. pet guinea pigs

2. **The name "guinea pig" is a mystery because:**
   a. their real name is a secret
   b. no one knows why they are called guinea pigs
   c. guinea pigs are scary

3. **Guinea pigs:**
   a. are all identical
   b. all have long hair
   c. come in many varieties

4. **The word "variety" means:**
   a. a show
   b. a message
   c. assortment

5. **To have a pet guinea pig you:**
   a. can live in the city or country
   b. must live in the country
   c. must have a big back yard

     FS-32046 **Reading**

Mynah Birds

The colorful mynah bird has a shiny black body, yellow legs and feet, and a bright orange beak. This bird is about the size of a small chicken. Mynah birds are very interesting pets. They need a cage, fresh water, mynah bird food and some fresh fruits. Grapes are a special treat for a mynah bird. Adults are fed once a day. When buying a pet, get a bird that is as young as possible. They can be purchased at six weeks of age. Mynah birds live to be about fifteen years old.

Showing off is typical of mynah birds. They are fun to watch. The Mynah can imitate voices. The first words are the hardest for them to learn. Once they start talking, they will quickly learn to say more. You can teach your bird to talk by saying words over and over in the same voice. You must be patient and practice with the bird every day. Both the male and female mynah can learn to be good talkers. They can change the way they talk and imitate several different people. A dog or cat can also be imitated by the mynah bird.

On a warm day let your mynah bird take a bath. A bowl of lukewarm, shallow water makes a perfect bird bath. The mynah bird will put on quite a show when taking its bath. You will probably have as much fun watching as the bird will have in its bath!

1. **A good title for this story is:**
   a. A Talking Bird
   b. Bird Houses
   c. Song Birds

2. **A mynah bird:**
   a. learns to talk by listening to others
   b. can only speak English
   c. learns to talk by itself

3. **The best way to teach your bird is:**
   a. to teach it many different things at once
   b. to practice the same lesson every day
   c. to practice the same lesson weekly

4. **The word "imitate" means:**
   a. frighten
   b. copy
   c. listen

5. **Mynah birds probably:**
   a. do not understand the meaning of what they say
   b. are shy
   c. can make up things to say

33   FS-32046 Reading

Blue Whale

The blue whale is the largest animal that ever lived. It is as long as eight elephants standing in a row. This gigantic animal eats tiny plants and animals in the sea. Isn't it strange that the largest animal eats food that is so small? There are two kinds of whales. One side of the whale family has teeth, and the other branch of the family is the toothless whale. Blue whales do not have teeth. Their throats are small and they cannot swallow anything large. The blue whale scoops up a giant mouthful of water, closes its mouth and then strains the water back out into the sea. A brush-like strainer called a baleen lets the water go out but holds in plants and animals for the whale to swallow.

Whales are not fish. They are mammals just like you. Mammals breathe air, are warm-blooded, have hair and drink milk from their mothers. Whales can drown if held under water. Their hair is just a few bristles.

The blue whale is an endangered species. There is concern that the blue whale may soon disappear forever. Too many have been hunted and killed by man. Now there are laws to protect the whales.

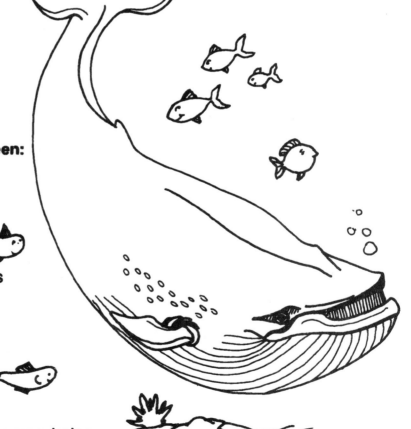

1. **The best title for this story is:**
   a. The Biggest Animal Ever
   b. A Large Fish
   c. All About Mammals

2. **The blue whale's enemy has been:**
   a. killer whales
   b. large ships
   c. man

3. **The whale family includes:**
   a. fish, crab and lobsters
   b. toothed and toothless whales
   c. only whales without teeth

4. **The word "endangered" means:**
   a. in danger
   b. not in danger
   c. protected

5. **Laws that protect whales:**
   a. make sure there aren't too many whales
   b. let whales live and reproduce
   c. are silly—whales can protect themselves

FS-32046 Reading

Name _____

Horses

Horses have helped people for many years. They pull carts, wagons, plows and carry people on their backs. Horses are beautiful, graceful animals. These powerful animals are gentle friends to people.

A horse needs a stable that is clean and dry. It needs some protection from extreme cold and heat. Horses need exercise. They eat hay and grain and drink lots of fresh water. Every day a horse needs grooming. Grooming includes brushing, combing and rubbing the shiny coat and cleaning its hoofs. It is important to remove small stones that may be caught in its hoofs. Horseshoes should be changed about once every six weeks. Horses are trained to obey their riders. When training a horse you must move slowly, talk quietly and not get upset. Your horse will understand that you are the boss and it will want to obey you. If you do not know how to ride you should get riding instructions. Busy streets are not good places to ride horses. Horses are frightened by sudden movements and noises and may bolt and run. Ride on trails or in open spaces where you can enjoy a view of the world from the strong back of a horse.

1. This story is mostly about:
   a. taming wild horses
   b. shoeing a horse
   c. caring for a horse

2. Horses:
   a. can make people's work easier
   b. have recently started helping people
   c. cannot do heavy work

3. Horses require:
   a. daily grooming
   b. new shoes yearly
   c. fresh meat to eat

4. The word "shiny" means the opposite of:
   a. glossy
   b. hairy
   c. dull

5. The horse:
   a. must be treated kindly
   b. will obey when shouted at
   c. must be trained by an adult

Mexico

Ana and Sergio are from Mexico, a warm country south of the United States. They have pet roosters, rabbits, goats, and a baby lamb. Mexican children, like children all over the world, love animals. Each year they have a special day called St. Anthony's Day when they take the pets to church to be blessed.

Sometimes the children go to village marketplaces to buy or trade products from their parent's farm. Other times they go to Mexico City where they shop in discount stores for bargains.

The people go to **fiestas** (parties) to celebrate holidays. They sing, dance and break **piñatas** (containers shaped like objects which are filled with candy, fruit and toys).

Some Mexican people still follow the old ways of life, but modern customs, schools, and houses are taking over. Mexico City is a center of education. Some Americans and Canadians study in Mexican universities.

The children play baseball and soccer. They watch bullfights and jai alai games.

Mexican people have given the world many beautiful works of art. In Mexico you might see pyramids like those in Egypt.

1. Mexico is a country just _____ of the United States.

2. The children in the story live on a _____ in Mexico.

3. _____ is a special day for people to have their pets blessed.

4. A _____ is a container filled with treats for use at _____ .

5. Children play _____ and _____ in Mexico.

6. You could take cool clothes and sandals if you visit Mexico because _____

_____ .

Individual Activities

1. Ask your teacher if you can weave, sing some Mexican songs or learn a Mexican dance. Draw a picture of a bookmark you could weave.
2. Read more about Mexico. Choose one subject to tell about in class.

Name _____

Japan

Kentaro was born in Japan. Japan is a country made up of four large islands and many small ones. It is located in the Pacific Ocean near China.

Kentaro lives in Tokyo, which is a large city. He lives in a huge apartment building. Kentaro usually wears clothes like yours. On special days his sister dresses in a long robe called a kimono, which is tied around the waist with a sash called an obi. At school Kentaro learns a special kind of writing done with a brush. He enjoys judo, but baseball is his favorite sport.

Kentaro likes to look at the cherry trees in bloom and enjoys special holidays like the Boys' Festival. His sister's favorite holiday is Girls' Day, the Festival of Dolls. His mother and her friends enjoy making beautiful flower arrangements. Kentaro thinks of Japan as a land of many mountains. One of the most famous mountains in the world is Japan's Mt. Fuji.

Kentaro likes to eat tacos and pizza now, but he still enjoys dishes made with rice, the main food in Japan.

1. Japan is a country made up of _____ in the _____ Ocean.

2. Kentaro's favorite sport is _____ .

3. The main food in Japan is _____ .

4. _____ is a famous mountain in Japan.

5. On special days, Kentaro's sister might wear a _____ tied

   with an _____ .

6. Today Kentaro likes to eat new foods like _____ and

   _____ .

Individual Activities

1. Read more about Japan. (You should choose one topic such as food, products, minerals, etc.) Locate the country on the map and tell your class some of the things you have learned.
2. Write a story about a day in Kentaro's life in Japan.

       FS-32046 **Reading**

Canada

Gordon is from Canada, the second largest country in the world. It is made up of provinces that are somewhat like states. Most of the Canadian people live within 200 miles of the U.S. border, because much of northern Canada is wilderness or **wasteland** (land that is not very useful for living on or for growing things).

Canada is a scenic land that attracts many tourists and has many natural resources which make it valuable for mining, fishing, forestry and manufacturing. It is one of the most successful countries in the world. Though it is an independent country, the King or Queen of Great Britain is also King or Queen of Canada. Since Canada shares common interests and backgrounds with the U.S., the two countries have been good friends for many years.

Hockey, baseball and football are popular sports in both countries. Being in Canada is somewhat like being in the United States, England, and France all at once, since the land was settled by the English and French. Both languages are spoken there.

1. Canada is a country similar to the U.S. that is made up of _____ .

2. _____ , _____ , and _____ are popular sports in Canada.

3. Canada is a very _____ land.

4. Most of the people live close to the _____ .

5. Land that is not useful to man may be called _____ .

6. Canadian customs are somewhat similar to customs in _____ ,

_____ and _____ .

Individual Activities

1. Use a travel folder or the encyclopedia to help you make a notebook of places to see in Canada.
2. Read about Quebec and see if you can see likenesses and differences between it and the rest of Canada.

Puerto Rico

Juan is from Puerto Rico, an island southwest of Florida. Puerto Rico means "rich port." The climate, its most important natural resource, brings visitors and allows a variety of crops to grow. There are many modern hotels there. People enjoy deep sea fishing and skin diving in this area.

Puerto Ricans are United States citizens and can move to the U.S. without permission. Perhaps by the time you read this Puerto Ricans may have decided to make their territory another state.

It is believed that Columbus discovered and landed on this island while sailing for Spain. The U.S. acquired Puerto Rico from Spain in 1898. Many people speak Spanish and celebrate with colorful festivals. Spanish music and art are popular. The U.S. government set up a public school system in Puerto Rico.

1. Puerto Rico is an island near _____ , U.S.A.

2. Many hotels are needed because Puerto Rico has many _____ .

3. Puerto Ricans can move to the U.S. without special permission because they

   are _____ .

4. Many customs of Puerto Rico are _____ , because the area was

   discovered by Columbus for _____ .

5. Another word for weather throughout the year is _____ .

6. Tourists probably choose Puerto Rico for a vacation because of the excellent

   _____ .

Individual Activities

1. Ask a travel agent for a pamphlet about Puerto Rico. Plan a pretend trip to the island. Tell how you would travel, what kind of clothes you would take, and what you would do there.
2. Draw a map of Puerto Rico. Show some important cities.

 FS-32046 Reading

Italy

Gina is from Italy, a country in Europe. Italy is one of the leading **tourist** (person making a tour or pleasure trip) centers of the world. Each year people travel to Italy to visit Roman ruins, monuments, beautiful churches, art museums and opera houses. The Leaning Tower of Pisa is one of the most famous tourist attractions in the world. Vatican City, home of the Pope and center of the Catholic Church, is another popular spot for visitors.

Vacationers may choose to spend time on the sunny beaches or travel to ski resorts in the Alps. They can enjoy gliding down the **canals** (waterways) of Venice in special boats called gondolas.

Gina loves to eat **pasta** (food made from a flour and water mixture) such as spaghetti or noodles. You would probably enjoy having dinner with her.

1. Italy is located in _____ .

2. The _____ is a famous tourist attraction.

3. People who visit another area for pleasure (fun) are called _____ .

4. You might enjoy riding in a special kind of boat called a _____ .

5. Five places where a visitor could learn about Italian history are _____ ,

_____ , _____ , _____ , or _____ .

6. Two opposite types of places you might choose for vacations in Italy are

_____ and _____ .

Individual Activities

1. Locate Pisa, Tower of, in an encyclopedia. Tell your class why it is leaning.
2. Read about a famous Italian artist such as Michaelangelo, da Vinci or Raphael. Write a report to share with your class.

Norway and Sweden

Kari and Sven's mother is from Norway, while their father is from Sweden. Both countries are in a part of northern Europe called Scandinavia. Part of each country is above the Arctic Circle. These countries are called "lands of the midnight sun" because during part of the summer the sun shines 24 hours a day. The area also has much snow, and skiing is a national sport. If you lived there you would probably learn to ski before you begin school.

The people of Norway do a lot of fishing and shipping. There are many long, narrow inlets where the sea reaches into the land called fjords. The land is high and rocky with little farmland. Rivers rushing down the mountainside provide cheap electricity for manufacturing. There are many famous writers, artists and musicians such as Edvard Grieg who came from this land.

Sweden is one of the most **prosperous** (successful) countries in the world. One famous way of serving meals is called the smörgasbörd, where a variety of cold and hot foods are put out for people to choose from. Perhaps you have been to a smörgasbörd. In school the children study subjects as you do, but everyone is also taught gymnastics. Many Americans buy Scandinavian furniture. Santa Lucia Day is a favorite holiday which reminds the people that Christmas is coming.

1. Two similar countries in Scandinavia are _____ and _____ .

2. If you wanted to choose from a variety of foods you might go to a _____ .

3. Fjords are common in _____ .

4. Many Americans buy Scandinavian _____ .

5. A word that means successful is _____ .

6. Since the sun shines all day and night during the summer, these countries have been

   nicknamed _____ .

Individual Activities

1. Use the encyclopedia to find out more about fjords. Then draw or paint a picture of a scene in Norway or Sweden.
2. Find out more about Edvard Grieg. See if you can get a record with some of his music to play for the class.

India

Seeta is a girl from India. India has more people than any other country except China, its northern neighbor. It is a land of **contrasts** including deserts, jungles, plains, mountains and lowlands. There are three seasons—hot, cold and rainy. The people are of many races and religions and speak about 180 languages. Some people wear ancient costumes, while others wear western clothes as you do. Sometimes people wear suits to work but change to traditional, loose clothing at home. Cloth wrapped around the head is called a turban. Women often wear a straight piece of cloth draped around the body as a long dress. This is called a sari.

India has large cities that are business and educational centers. It also has many small villages with mud and straw homes and very small schools.

Music is played on instruments somewhat like guitars but with more strings. Their music sounds different to us because they play complicated melodies instead of chords. Dancers tell stories with their hands and fingers. Beautiful carvings are made from stone and ivory.

1. India is a country of many people and a land of _____ .

2. Some people prefer both the _____ and _____ ways of life.

3. Stories are told by dancers using their _____ and _____ .

4. A cloth wrapped around the head is called a _____ , while one draped

   around the body like a dress is called a _____ .

5. In the story, the word "contrasts" means _____ .

6. Because of the many different languages spoken it might be hard for some Indian

   people to _____ each other.

Individual Activities

1. Use an encyclopedia to find a map showing the products of India. Make a product map to share with your class.
2. See if your public library has any recordings of Indian music. Play the records for for your class.

FS-32046 Reading

Cuba

Lupe and Roberto live in Cuba. Cuba is located south of Florida and is the largest island in the West Indies. It was discovered by Columbus, who is said to have called it "the loveliest land human eyes have beheld (seen)."

The people grow sugar cane, tobacco, and vegetables. Cuban mines produce minerals such as manganese, iron, copper, platinum and gold. The climate is pleasantly warm, but hurricanes often hit the area.

Most of the people are of Spanish backgrounds and eat Spanish food.

Lupe and Roberto enjoy watching sports like jai alai, soccer, baseball, polo, horse racing, golf, and swimming. The waters around Cuba contain many big fish such as marlin, barracuda, shark, and swordfish.

1. Cuba is a large island south of _____ in the West Indies.

2. The island was said by Columbus to be very _____ .

3. Some products grown there include _____ .

4. One weather problem this area has is _____ .

5. "Behold" means to _____ .

6. The customs in Cuba are probably similar to those in _____ countries.

Individual Activities

1. Find out about the game jai alai. Explain the game to your class.
2. Read more about Cuba today. How has it changed?

---

43   FS-32046 Reading

Israel

Moishe grew up in Israel, a country in the Middle East. Most of the mountains, rivers and cities still have the same names they had in Biblical times. The Jewish people returned to this land in 1948 and have worked hard to build a modern nation. They lost their land many years ago. All Jewish people are welcome to move to Israel.

The Israelis celebrate most of the same holidays that Jewish children everywhere celebrate. They also have tree-planting ceremonies where you may have a tree planted in memory of someone you knew.

The people speak Hebrew or Arabic, and some English. Although Israel is in the Middle East, the cities and towns seem more like western cities in North America or Europe.

The people of Israel eat mostly bread, grains, fruit and dairy products. Many of the people work in manufacturing or farming. Often families and friends work together and share the profits on one large farm known as a kibbutz. Each person has his or her special job. Some do the farming while others care for the children or do different work.

1. Although the _____ people were once sent out of Israel, they have come back to build their nation.

2. Israelis probably eat _____ (more, less) meat than we do.

3. To honor someone you may _____ in Israel.

4. Three languages spoken in Israel are _____ .

5. A farm shared by several families or people is called a _____ .

6. The Jewish people probably were willing to fight and work hard because they wanted

_____ .

Individual Activities

1. In an encyclopedia find the Israeli flag. Draw a picture of it. Tell your class what the colors and symbols stand for.
2. Watch the newspaper for articles telling about Israel today. Share one article with your class.

Samoa

Saru's parents came from the island of Samoa in the Pacific Ocean about five thousand miles southwest of California. Most of the islands in that area were formed by volcanoes and are surrounded by coral reefs.

The climate is pleasant, except for periods between January and March when gales and hurricanes sweep in.

The people sell **copra** (the meat of coconuts), cacao, and bananas to other countries. Sending products to other countries is called "exporting."

The people are Polynesians as are the Hawaiian people. "Polynesia" means "many islands." Some people of Samoa carry on ancient ways and crafts. They may dress in colorful costumes and paint their faces. They do fascinating island dances. In Hawaii you can visit the Polynesian Cultural Center and see sample homes that show you how the Samoan people live. You may also see a Polynesian dancing show. The people are graceful, athletic, and love water sports such as swimming, diving and surfing. Saru wears a simple cloth wrapped around his body from his waist to his ankles. It is called a lavalava. The people still make tapa cloth by beating the bark of paper mulberry trees. It is used for clothing and decorating houses.

1. Another name for the Pacific islands is _____ .

2. It might be hard to reach some of the islands because they are surrounded by _____

   _____ .

3. In their spare time the people enjoy _____ .

4. Polynesians make tapa cloth from _____ .

5. _____ means to send products to other countries for sale or trade.

6. January through March would not be the best time to visit Samoa because of

   _____ and _____ .

Individual Activities

1. Look up "coral reef." Tell your class what you learned.
2. Borrow the book "The Cay" from a library. If it is too hard for you to read, have a parent or your teacher read it to you or the class.

       FS-32046 Reading

Brazil

Rosa is from Brazil, the largest country in South America. Her country supplies the world with such products as coffee, sugar cane, minerals, lumber, cattle, hogs, cotton, and cacao beans from which we make chocolate and cocoa. Much of the country's trade is done with the United States. It is a modern country. Most of the people live near the Atlantic Ocean.

The majority of people speak Portuguese, since Portugal received the land from Spain in 1494. Soccer, the favorite sport in Brazil, is becoming a favorite in North America too. Pelé, a famous player from Brazil, also played in the United States.

Rosa wears a white blouse and dark skirt to school, much as students do in some schools in other countries. When school is not in session she loves to go to the beach. Sometimes Rosa and other Brazilians prefer to sleep in hammocks which are made of cloth or straw and are hung by the ends from walls or posts. Modern hotels may offer hammocks instead of beds.

There are many offices and hotels. They are often decorated with bright colored tiles. Artists there are now painting very modern designs.

The great Amazon River winds through the jungles of Brazil. This river has more water than any other river. Big game hunters search the area for jaguars, mountain lions and crocodiles. You may have seen this jungle area in movies or television.

1. Brazil is the _____ country in South America and supplies the world with

   many _____ .

2. The chocolate you eat probably began as _____ beans.

3. The favorite sport is _____ .

4. The _____ is an extremely large and important river.

5. A lounge or bed hung from the ends is called a _____ .

6. Before the people spoke Portuguese, the language in Brazil was probably

   _____ .

Individual Activities

1. Begin a flag book. Draw the flag of Brazil for your book.
2. Write a short story or play about a trip to Brazil. How would you get there? What would you see and do? Use ideas from the story, encyclopedia, or travel folders.

     FS-32046 Reading

Peru

Alma is from Peru in South America. Peru is on the Pacific Ocean side of South America and is about three times as big as California. Alma is looking forward to Independence Day which is in July. There will be parades, music, fireworks and a special family dinner with duckling and rice.

Alma's parents have a small farm in the valley. Her grandparents live high in the mountains and herd cattle, sheep and llamas. Their home is made of adobe (sun dried clay bricks) and has a red tile roof. They have less furniture than most Americans have in their homes. When school is over Alma loves to jump rope.

The clothes worn in Peru near the coast may be much like yours. In the mountains they wear woolen clothing. A blanket-like covering with a hole in the middle is worn over other clothes to keep warm. It is called a poncho.

Peru was once the land of the Inca Indians. Parts of ancient Inca cities are still in the mountains of Peru. Later Spanish soldiers conquered the country. Peruvians may have both Indian and Spanish ancestors.

The mountains of Peru are rich in minerals including copper, gold, silver, iron, lead and zinc. Perhaps you have some jewelry made of silver from Peru.

1. Peru is a large country in _____ near the _____ Ocean.

2. If you wanted to visit Inca cities, you would probably go to the _____ of Peru.

3. Some minerals we might get from Peru are _____ .

4. For cold weather, children and adults can put on their _____ .

5. Sun dried clay is called _____ .

6. Since the country had many Indians and Spanish, it is likely most people can speak

   either _____ or _____ .

Individual Activities

1. Look for llama in the dictionary. Draw a llama.
2. Read about the Inca Indians. Write a report and tell your class what you learned.

47

woman	mother	heart	elder sister	younger sister

China

Mei Ling's family is from China. It is near Russia, India and Japan. China has the largest population of any country in the world. Most people are farmers who grow China's food supply. Rice is the main food. Rice dishes made with pork or chicken are favorites. They irrigate their fields by bringing water from streams or rivers.

The Chinese people were the first to develop gunpowder, paper, porcelain, printing and silk cloth.

Though many people live in villages, new city areas have modern offices, factories, stores and apartments.

Chinese art began before history was written. The ancient Chinese made beautiful carved jade and stone, bronze statues, porcelain ware, painted scrolls, etc.

In school, children may learn to read and write the interesting Chinese symbols with a brush. The children love to celebrate the Chinese New Year. They celebrate all night and welcome the New Year with fireworks. They may receive gifts and coins.

1. China has more _____ than any other country.

2. Chinese people were the first to develop such things as _____ ,

_____ , _____ , _____ and _____ .

3. Most people earn a living by _____ .

4. _____ is the main food and can be made into a special dish by adding

_____ or _____ .

5. To bring water to an area for farming is called _____ .

6. The more people a country has, the more _____ it must grow or get in trade
   from other countries.

Individual Activities

1. Find pictures of Chinese art work in a book or encyclopedia. Sketch some of them or make a Chinese type painting of your own.
2. Ask your teacher if he or she can invite someone to talk about China, or find an article about China today in the newspaper and tell your class what you have learned.

     FS-32046 Reading

Egypt

Hassan and Zainab are from Egypt, a country that borders on the Mediterranean and Red Seas. Since Egypt is mainly a desert area, the people depend on the Nile River which provides most of the water and rich soil. The River is a **natural resource** (something in nature that is helpful to man).

Often children help their parents with farm work. They go to school to learn to read and write their language. Some children learn to make bronze objects or food items such as butter and cheese. They enjoy hopscotch and games like marbles, played with pebbles.

Long ago huge pyramids were built in Egypt as tombs, or burial places, for dead kings. Many beautiful things were found in tombs like that of King Tut.

1. Egyptians depend strongly on the _____ .

2. Tombs are special places for people who are _____ .

3. The Nile River provides both _____ and _____ .

4. The children use pebbles to play a game like _____ .

5. A _____ is something provided by nature that is useful to man.

6. A good place for a farm in Egypt would be near the _____ .

Individual Activities

1. Read about Egyptian art or the King Tut Treasures. Make some sketches of their art objects or paintings.
2. Use an encyclopedia to find out what products are produced in Egypt. What product do the Arab countries have that Egypt and so many countries need?

 FS-32046 Reading

Panama

Miguel is from Panama. Panama is located in Central America, just north of South America. Years ago the United States built a waterway between the Pacific and Atlantic Oceans called the Panama Canal. Now ships do not have to travel all the way around South America to carry goods. The United States Congress voted to give the canal to the Panamanian people.

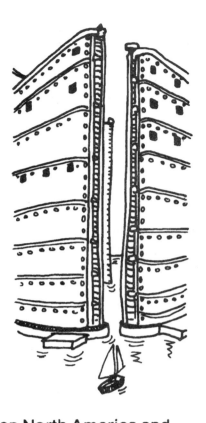

The climate in Panama is generally hot with a great deal of rain. Most of the people speak Spanish, but many speak English as you do.

Rice, corn, and beans are the main foods eaten in Panama. Miguel's mother grinds the corn and makes paste for tortillas.

The people wear lightweight clothes much like you wear in warm weather. On special days the people have celebrations called fiestas, and the women wear long dresses with beautiful embroidery. The men wear loose embroidered shirts.

1. Panama is located in _____ which is between North America and

   _____ .

2. A canal is a _____ between two places.

3. Most people in Panama speak _____ , though many speak _____ .

4. The Panama Canal is important because it connects the _____ and

   _____ Oceans.

5. A food made from ground corn is a _____ .

6. Panamanians wear lightweight clothing because _____ .

Individual Activities

1. Read about the Panama Canal. Draw a map showing its location. Tell why it is so important.
2. Watch the newspaper for articles about Panama and the Canal.

     FS-32046 Reading

Great Britain

Anne and Alan live in Great Britain. Great Britain includes England, Scotland, Wales and Northern Ireland. In England you can visit London and see the famous tower clock, Big Ben. You might go on a fox hunt, and of course you would stay for afternoon tea. In Northern Ireland you would view the beautiful green countryside that gives the country the nickname "Emerald Isle." You might listen to a storyteller telling folktales about fairies or leprechauns. In Scotland you could visit a clan gathering where a group of related families gather for fun. Some of the men would be wearing kilts, which are skirt-like garments made of the special clan plaid. They play the bagpipes and do a country dance such as the Highland Fling.

1. Great Britain includes _____ , _____ ,

 _____ and _____ .

2. In London you could see a tower clock called _____ .

3. In the afternoon the English drink _____ .

4. In Scotland they play an instrument called a _____ .

5. You might visit a clan gathering in _____ .

6. "Emerald Isle" is another name for _____ .

Individual Activities

1. Have your classmates find out where their ancestors lived. Mark these countries on a world map with the classmate's name.
2. Read and tell or write about the native country of one of your ancestors. Make a display of the reports for Open House.

Nigeria

Kehinde is from Nigeria in Western Africa, a country of many people and unusual animals. It is a land of **contrasts** (big differences) with very rainy areas as well as hot dry areas. Nigeria has the largest population in Africa.

Many languages are spoken in Nigeria including English, which is taught in most schools. The government is working to develop the natural resources and to improve schools. It is one of Africa's largest oil producers.

Nigerians produce many crops. Plows and oxen are often used instead of modern farm machinery. Some people are nomads who move from place to place. They live mainly in desert areas herding camels, goats and sheep. They may live in tents or homes made of branches and plants. Some families live and work together in groups called tribes, sharing old ways.

New apartments and office buildings make the big cities much like ours. The people may dress as we do, or they may wear long flowing robes. Women sometimes cover their faces with veils. People in very hot areas wear little clothing.

Many famous legends and folktales come from this land. Its music has a powerful beat of drums.

1. Nigeria is a land of _____ with rainy and _____ areas.

2. Nigeria has the _____ population in Africa.

3. Nigeria is one of Africa's largest producers of _____ .

4. Nomads are people who _____ from place to place.

5. People who live and work together in groups are called _____ .

6. Two other names for stories are _____ and _____ .

Individual Activities

1. Read about the plants and animals of this area. Plan a pretend trip to Africa. Perhaps it will be a safari. Draw pictures of what you will see.
2. Read an African folktale to your class. Perhaps your library has records with African folktales or legends you can share.

 FS-32046 Reading

Name _____

 # American Indian—Navajo

Sam's ancestors were the first Americans. These people are called Indians, because Columbus thought he had reached India. There are many different tribes of Indians who live in different ways.

Sam's tribe, the Navajo, lives in the southwestern United States. It is believed that they came to Arizona and New Mexico from Canada. The Pueblo Indians taught the Navajo to grow corn, weave, and make sand paintings. Many Navajo artists paint murals and water colors. Beautiful designs are used for jewelry, pottery, weaving, and clothing.

Some Navajo Indians prefer to follow the old ways. Most of them live, at least part of the time, on land set aside by the government called reservations. Many people work there, farming, raising cattle, doing craft work, etc. Others may work in nearby factories, mines or at professions such as teaching or medicine.

1. The Indian originally received that name from _____ who believed he had

   reached _____ .

2. Indians today may still live on _____ if they wish to do so.

3. A reservation is an area of _____ .

4. The _____ Indians live in the _____ United States.

5. Beautiful Navajo designs are used today in _____ , _____ ,

   _____ and _____ , etc.

6. Some Indian tribes taught other tribes much as the Indians taught white settlers. The

   Pueblo Indians taught the Navajo Indians to _____ , _____ and

   make _____ .

Individual Activities

1. Find a copy of a poem about Indians such as "Hiawatha" by Longfellow. Practice reading the poem aloud. Read it to your class.
2. Locate **Indians** in your encyclopedia. Get ideas about Indian designs. Try drawing the designs on paper or clay.

Vietnam

Kim is from Vietnam. The country is near China. The people of Kim's country have similarities to the people of China or Japan. Both countries had a great influence on Vietnam. Many people are rice farmers and live in small villages near river deltas. Some farmers still use simple wooden plows pulled by animals. Rice is the main crop. More people now live in cities. They are businessmen, shopkeepers, or merchants.

The people value education and are training skilled workers. They are encouraging people to attend universities.

There are many forests in Vietnam. A variety of minerals can be found in the country. Rice and rubber are important exports.

1. Vietnam is similar to _____ and _____ .

2. Some of the people live in _____ near _____ .

3. Some important products exported from Vietnam are _____ .

   and _____ .

4. Farmers may still use _____ .

5. Vietnam is encouraging more people to attend _____ .

6. People who live in the cities might be _____ ,

   _____ or _____ .

Individual Activities

1. See if anyone in your class has relatives from this country. Invite those persons to give a talk about the country. Encourage people from different countries to visit your classroom to talk about their land of birth.
2. Look at a map of Vietnam. Draw an outline of the country.

Wonder Woman

Some sports writers thought Babe **Didrikson** was the best **athlete** that ever lived. Babe Didrikson could play almost any sport well. She played basketball, baseball, football, and tennis. She also swam, bowled and even did some boxing.

Babe Didrikson played on the All-America women's basketball team in 1931 and 1932. She often scored 30 points or more in a game. Babe also won two gold medals in track and set world records at the Olympics. She loved playing any sport but became most famous as a golfer.

Babe began playing golf in the late 1930's. She set a record by winning seventeen women's golf matches in a row. She was the first American woman to win the British Women's golf match. She won 82 matches in all.

In 1954, Babe Didrikson was named the best woman in sports from 1900 to 1950.

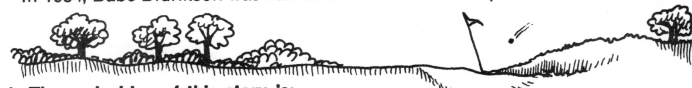

1. **The main idea of this story is:**
   a. Babe Didrikson played a lot of baseball.
   b. Babe Didrikson could play almost any sport well.
   c. Babe Didrikson got two gold medals.

2. **People thought that:**
   a. Babe couldn't play golf.
   b. Babe was a strange name.
   c. Babe was the best woman ever in sports.

3. **How many golf matches did Babe Didrikson win?**
   a. 82
   b. 98
   c. 86

4. **The word <u>athlete</u> means:**
   a. a brave person
   b. a person who plays sports well
   c. someone who reads a lot

5. **The story does not say, but Babe Didrikson was probably good at sports because:**
   a. She studied math.
   b. She ran every day.
   c. She was very strong.

Ten-Fingered Wizard

As a child José **Feliciano** listened to the radio. Music became his whole world. José was born blind and could not do a lot of things other children could do. While other children were playing outside, José learned to play the guitar and sing. He also learned to play the banjo, conga drums, harmonica, piano and organ. He couldn't read music so he learned to play by ear.

José began performing on the guitar for people when he was seventeen. One man called José a "ten-fingered wizard". His first big record was "Light My Fire". He won many awards for his songs. José wrote the title song for the television series, "Chico and the Man". That song also became popular.

Today José Feliciano performs all over the world. His blindness doesn't stop him from doing things anymore. He has learned to swim, sail a boat, play baseball and ride bicycles.

1. **The main idea of this story is:**
   a. José Feliciano owns a radio.
   b. José Feliciano is an actor.
   c. José Feliciano plays the guitar well.

2. **José Feliciano:**
   a. can play many different instruments
   b. lives in England
   c. enjoys skydiving

3. **One of José Feliciano's big record hits was:**
   a. Ten-Fingered Wizard
   b. Light My Fire
   c. All Over the World

4. **To <u>play by ear</u> means:**
   a. to put your ear on a piano
   b. to make music with your ears
   c. to hear music and be able to play it

5. **Being blind and learning to play an instrument is probably:**
   a. very hard
   b. very easy
   c. done by many people

Pioneer Girl

Laura Ingalls Wilder was born in a log cabin on the edge of the Big Woods of **Wisconsin** in 1867. When she was still a baby, the family traveled West by covered wagon. Laura grew up on the prairie and went to school in a one-room schoolhouse. She became a teacher when she was sixteen and later married Almanzo Wilder.

Laura Wilder wrote about her life in the "Little House" books. Each book told about the sadness and joys of pioneer life. "Little House in the Big Woods" told about her childhood. "Farmer Boy" is the story of Almanzo Wilder's childhood. "These Happy Golden Years" describes the first years of Laura and Almanzo's marriage and the birth of their daughter Rose.

Laura Wilder received many prizes for her books. The "Little House" books were so popular, they were made into a television series.

Laura Wilder lived on a farm in **Missouri** until her death in 1957. She was 90 years old.

1. **The main idea of this story is:**
   a. Laura lived in a log cabin.
   b. Laura wrote books about her life.
   c. Laura lived to be 90 years old.

2. **Laura's school was:**
   a. painted white
   b. very large
   c. very small

3. **Laura's family were:**
   a. bankers
   b. sailors
   c. pioneers

4. **The word describes means:**
   a. tells about
   b. becomes sad
   c. runs around

5. **Since Laura Wilder lived a long time:**
   a. She traveled around the world.
   b. She met the president.
   c. She saw many changes in the world.

The Sad-Faced Clown

He wore ragged clothes and always looked like he was just about to cry. Yet "Weary Willie" made children laugh for over 40 years. The man behind Weary Willie's clown face was Emmett Kelly. Emmett joined the circus in 1933 and soon after became a clown.

Emmett decided he wanted to be a very special clown. He didn't want to wear white face make-up. So Emmett invented the character "Weary Willie". Emmett made up his face with a dark beard and a large pink nose. He also drew a large turned-down mouth on his face. He dressed as a hobo in old, torn clothes.

The character Weary Willie never talked. Sometimes he pretended to sweep the circus ring with a broom. He tried to sweep away the spotlight, but it kept moving away from him. Other times, he tried to crack a peanut with an ax. Emmett performed with the Ringling Brothers, Barnum and Bailey Circus. His son, Emmett Kelly, Jr., also became a clown.

1. The main idea of this story is:
   a. Emmett Kelly was a sad man.
   b. Emmett Kelly drew pictures.
   c. Emmett Kelly was a clown.

2. Most clowns wear:
   a. white face make-up
   b. ragged clothes
   c. sad faces

3. As a clown, Emmett called himself:
   a. Sad Sack
   b. Weepy Walter
   c. Weary Willie

4. A spotlight is:
   a. a light that has spots on it
   b. a light that moves and shines on one thing
   c. a light spot on your clothes

5. People love clowns because:
   a. They do funny things.
   b. They all live in Boston.
   c. They are good swimmers.

Finding a Cure

In the 1950's, polio was a dangerous illness. Every year many people became crippled or died because of polio. Then in 1953, Dr. Jonas Salk said he had found a cure. His medicine was made in the form of a **vaccine**. The vaccine was given by a shot. First Salk and his family took the medicine. The vaccine was found to be safe. Then almost two million school children were given polio shots in 1954. Soon people were not afraid of getting polio anymore.

In 1960, Dr. Albert Sabin made a stronger polio vaccine. He put it on sugar cubes. People didn't have to take polio shots anymore. They could eat their medicine. The Sabin vaccine lasted longer than the Salk vaccine. Thanks to these two men, polio has almost disappeared.

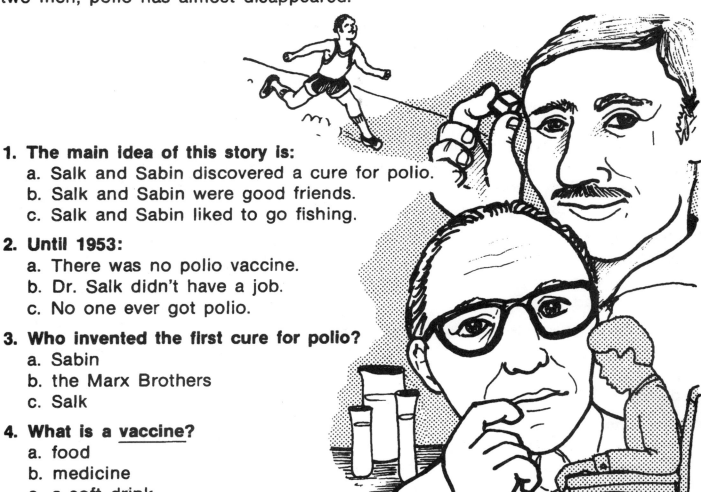

1. **The main idea of this story is:**
   a. Salk and Sabin discovered a cure for polio.
   b. Salk and Sabin were good friends.
   c. Salk and Sabin liked to go fishing.

2. **Until 1953:**
   a. There was no polio vaccine.
   b. Dr. Salk didn't have a job.
   c. No one ever got polio.

3. **Who invented the first cure for polio?**
   a. Sabin
   b. the Marx Brothers
   c. Salk

4. **What is a <u>vaccine</u>?**
   a. food
   b. medicine
   c. a soft drink

5. **If Salk and Sabin had not found a cure for polio:**
   a. Many people would still get sick from polio.
   b. People would not like them.
   c. Salk and Sabin would have bought a restaurant.

Beatles Forever

The Beatles were probably the most popular group in rock music history. They changed rock music by using pretty tunes and interesting words. They also brought long hair into fashion. Because of their hair, they were also called the "mop tops". George Harrison, John Lennon, Paul McCartney and Ringo Starr were all born in Liverpool, England. They began performing in the early 60's. In 1962, they made their first record and by 1964, they had become world-famous. Some of their early hits were "Please, Please Me", and "I Wanna Hold Your Hand".

The Beatles toured the United States several times. They were greeted everywhere by fans who loved them and their music. The Beatles starred in two movies, "A Hard Day's Night" and "Help!"

The group broke up in 1970, but by that time they had sold more records than any other performers in popular music.

1. **The main idea of this story is:**
   a. The Beatles were a very popular music group.
   b. The Beatles made movies.
   c. The Beatles were born in Liverpool.

2. **The Beatles were called the "mop tops" because:**
   a. They carried mops and tops.
   b. They were very neat.
   c. They had long hair.

3. **What kind of music did the Beatles play?**
   a. jazz
   b. rock
   c. country western

4. **The word <u>famous</u> means:**
   a. funny
   b. well-known
   c. smart

5. **You can tell that the Beatles' movies were probably:**
   a. silly
   b. long
   c. popular

Seeing in the Dark

When Anne Sullivan first met Helen Keller, Helen acted more like a wild animal than a child. At age two, before she learned to talk, Helen became very ill. The illness destroyed her sight and hearing. Helen never learned to talk. She could only make angry sounds or happy sounds. But Anne Sullivan was a very good teacher. After much hard work, she taught Helen to talk through sign language. Later, Helen learned to read and write **Braille**, the written language of the blind. Finally, when she was sixteen, Helen learned to speak.

Helen went to college. After finishing school, she began working to help the blind and the deaf-blind. She gave lectures, wrote books and visited the President of the United States. During World War II, she worked with soldiers who had been blinded in the war.

The motion picture, "The **Miracle** Worker", is based on Helen Keller's early life.

1. **The main idea of this story is:**
   a. Anne Sullivan was a good teacher.
   b. Helen liked college.
   c. Helen learned to overcome her problems.

2. **Until she was sixteen, Helen:**
   a. did not go to school
   b. could not talk
   c. did not eat spinach

3. **Helen learned to read:**
   a. Braille
   b. Morse Code
   c. print

4. **What does <u>destroyed</u> mean?**
   a. to find
   b. to freeze
   c. to ruin

5. **Helen probably wanted to help the blind because:**
   a. She thought it was interesting.
   b. She was blind herself.
   c. She liked hard work.

Square People

Some of the figures he drew had two noses, crossed eyes and twisted bodies. Yet Pablo **Picasso** is thought to be one of the most important artists of this century.

Picasso was born in Spain, but lived in France from 1904 until his death. His early drawings were simple. People looked like people and trees looked like trees. But soon Picasso began to experiment with his art. For a time he only used the color blue in his paintings. Then he began drawing figures that looked more like squares and triangles than people. He used dark colors and printed words in his paintings.

In 1937, The town **Guenerica** was destroyed in the Spanish Civil War. Picasso painted a picture called "Guenerica" as a protest against the war. It became his most famous painting.

Picasso's later paintings were easier to understand. Today his paintings hang in almost every large museum in the world.

1. The main idea of this story is:
   a. Picasso was an important artist.
   b. Picasso moved a lot.
   c. Picasso lived in France.

2. At one time, Picasso:
   a. only used one color in his paintings
   b. wrote many books
   c. was a school teacher

3. Picasso was born in:
   a. France
   b. England
   c. Spain

4. What does <u>twisted</u> mean?
   a. dark
   b. crooked
   c. cold

5. Most artists probably:
   a. do not always draw like Picasso
   b. do not draw pictures
   c. do not paint

Wilt the Stilt

Wilt **Chamberlain** is over seven feet tall. But he also stands tall as a fine basketball player. He set some records that have never been broken. During the 1961-62 season, he made more than 4,000 points. In one game he scored 100 points.

He was always a great player but people used to call him a loser. Even though he made a lot of points every game, his teams used to lose. People said he didn't care about his teams, but he did. In 1967, he proved that he could be a good team player too. Wilt was playing with the **Philadelphia** 76ers. He helped them win the championship. He didn't make a lot of points himself. But he helped keep the ball away from the other team.

In 1970 he joined the Los Angeles Lakers. He helped them win the championship in 1972. Wilt Chamberlain was voted best player of the year three times in a row.

1. The main idea of this story is:
   a. Wilt Chamberlain is very tall.
   b. Wilt didn't want to play for the Philadelphia 76ers.
   c. Wilt was a great basketball player.

2. Chamberlain was called "Wilt the Stilt" because:
   a. He stood on stilts.
   b. He was always jumping up and down.
   c. He was very tall.

3. What was the most points Wilt scored during one game?
   a. 250
   b. 100
   c. 75

4. What does <u>scored</u> mean?
   a. made points
   b. bought food
   c. hit the ball

5. Wilt was voted best player of the year because:
   a. He was the tallest man on his team.
   b. He helped his team win.
   c. He ran very fast.

Woman of Two Worlds

Maria Tallchief is an **Osage** Indian. Her father was a chief, but her family did not practice the Indian ways. However, her grandmother Elizabeth Bigheart told Maria many stories about their tribe.

Maria began taking dance lessons when she was four years old. She practiced very hard and became a good dancer. She learned to jump high in the air and dance on her toes. When she was eighteen she joined a ballet company. She was asked to change her name because it did not sound like a dancer's name. But Maria was very proud to be an Indian and kept her name.

Soon she became very famous. A dance was made just for her. It was called "The Firebird". Maria played a beautiful bird with magic powers. Everyone thought Maria was wonderful in the part.

The Osage people made Maria a princess and called her "The Woman of Two Worlds". Although Maria lived far from her people, she always remembered them.

1. The main idea of this story is:
   a. Maria Tallchief played the piano.
   b. Maria Tallchief was a firebird.
   c. Maria Tallchief was a great dancer.

2. Ballet dancers dance:
   a. on their toes
   b. in the water
   c. on table tops

3. What was the name of Maria's tribe?
   a. Two Worlds
   b. Bigheart
   c. Osage

4. What does <u>remember</u> mean?
   a. to forget about
   b. to go to
   c. to think of

5. Maria probably became a good dancer because:
   a. She played the bongo drums.
   b. She practiced every day.
   c. She owned a dancing school.

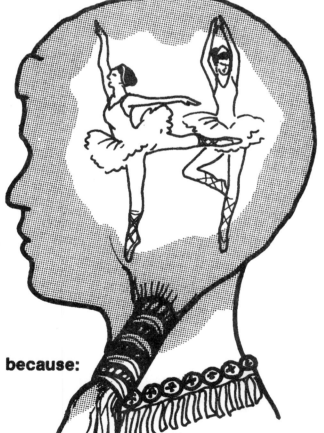

 **Get a Horse**

People laughed at the first cars. They ran on steam and were very noisy. They spilled smoke and hot coals into the air. Then the electric car was developed in 1890. It was quiet and did not dirty the air. But it could not travel more than 20 miles per hour. Also, the car's batteries had to be charged every 50 miles.

Gradually, the gasoline-powered car became the most popular. Henry Ford developed one of these cars. It had a single seat, bicycle wheels and an electric bell.

The early cars were very expensive. But Henry Ford believed that everyone should have a car. His factory began to make cars more quickly and at less cost. His most popular car was the Model T. It only cost $400.

Henry Ford developed the V-8 engine. It is a very strong engine that is still used in cars today. Henry spent the last part of his life working to help other people.

1. The main idea of this story is:
   a. The first airplanes were very funny-looking.
   b. Henry Ford developed new cars.
   c. Henry Ford's first car had an electric bell.

2. Electric cars were:
   a. too slow
   b. too fast
   c. too ugly

3. What kind of engine did the first cars have?
   a. gasoline
   b. electric
   c. steam

4. What does <u>expensive</u> mean?
   a. something very big
   b. something that costs a lot of money
   c. something very cold to eat

5. If people still drove electric cars:
   a. We would run out of water.
   b. The air would be very dirty.
   c. It would take longer to get places.

A World Without Sun

Jacques **Cousteau** sails around the world on his ship **Calypso**. He films the underwater world. He has shown seals playing in the water and seagulls hunting for their dinner. He has filmed walruses floating on icebergs in the Arctic. Jacques has also shown sharks sleeping in caves in Mexico. On one trip he even found a Greek ship that had been buried under the sea for over 2,000 years.

Jacques Cousteau believes that someday man will live under the oceans. In 1963 he tried to prove that was possible. He and four divers lived in an underwater house for one month. The house was filled with air so the men could breathe.

Jacques Cousteau loves the ocean and all its living things. He gets very angry when people dump oil and garbage in it. He does everything he can do to protect it. Once he stopped France from dumping dangerous materials in the ocean.

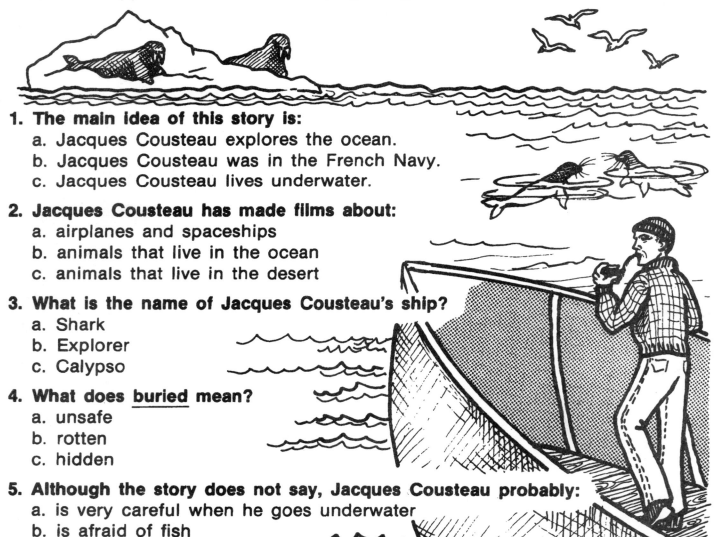

1. **The main idea of this story is:**
   a. Jacques Cousteau explores the ocean.
   b. Jacques Cousteau was in the French Navy.
   c. Jacques Cousteau lives underwater.

2. **Jacques Cousteau has made films about:**
   a. airplanes and spaceships
   b. animals that live in the ocean
   c. animals that live in the desert

3. **What is the name of Jacques Cousteau's ship?**
   a. Shark
   b. Explorer
   c. Calypso

4. **What does <u>buried</u> mean?**
   a. unsafe
   b. rotten
   c. hidden

5. **Although the story does not say, Jacques Cousteau probably:**
   a. is very careful when he goes underwater
   b. is afraid of fish
   c. only eats seaweed

Name _____ Date _____

He Searched for His Past

When Alex Haley was a boy, his grandmother used to tell him stories about their family. She told Alex about his long-dead ancestor, **Kunta Kinte**. Kunta Kinte had come to America on a slave ship. Alex Haley decided that one day he would write the story of his family.

Many years later Alex Haley decided he was ready to write about his family. He spent twelve years studying his family history. He went to Africa and searched for his relatives. He found the Kinte family.

Alex Haley's book was called <u>Roots</u>. It told how Kunta Kinte tried to escape to freedom. He also wrote about Kunta's daughter, Kizzy, who was one of the few slaves who could read and write. Alex wrote stories about his other ancestors all the way down to his father. Alex wrote stories about himself, too.

<u>Roots</u> was made into a television motion picture. It was one of the most popular movies in television history.

1. The main idea of this story is:
   a. Alex Haley was a boy.
   b. Alex Haley's grandmother was a good storyteller.
   c. Alex Haley wrote the story of his family.

2. Kunta Kinte was a:
   a. slave
   b. farmer
   c. sailor

3. What was the name of Alex Haley's book?
   a. Family
   b. Roots
   c. Kunta Kinte

4. What are <u>relatives</u>?
   a. family members
   b. visitors
   c. friends

5. Alex Haley probably decided to find out about his family because:
   a. He wanted to find out where he came from.
   b. His mother told him to do it.
   c. The government wanted to know.

     FS-32046 Reading

Name _____ Date _____

A Real Winner

Billie Jean King began playing tennis after school when she was eleven. She decided then that she was going to be a winner. She worked very hard. Soon she became one of America's best young tennis players.

Billie Jean King began to play in important tennis matches and she usually won. She won first place at the United States Open three times. She also won first place at the **Wimbledon** Matches in England six times.

In 1973, she faced one of the most important tennis matches of her life. Tennis player Bobby Riggs said women's tennis was just a big joke. He said he could beat the best woman tennis player. And Billie Jean was the best. She agreed to play against him.

On September 20, 1973, Billie Jean King met Bobby Riggs in the **Astrodome** in **Houston, Texas**. People all over the United States watched the game on television. The Astrodome was crowded with people. When Billie Jean won, the crowd cheered and cheered.

1. The main idea of this story is:
   a. Billie Jean King likes to tell jokes.
   b. Billie Jean King was a great tennis player.
   c. Bobby Riggs likes to knit.

2. Bobby Riggs thought:
   a. Women weren't as good tennis players as men.
   b. He was the best football player in the world.
   c. He could swim faster than any woman.

3. The Astrodome is in:
   a. Paris
   b. Houston
   c. New York

4. The word crowded means:
   a. empty
   b. full
   c. wet

5. Billie Jean King believed that:
   a. Women's tennis was important.
   b. Bobby Riggs should go back to school.
   c. Tennis was a silly game.

       FS-32046 Reading

Clowning Around

On the screen, the Marx Brothers moved like a whirlwind. Groucho chomped on his cigar and made jokes. Chico pretended to speak **Italian**. Harpo chased people around the room. They wore silly clothes and did crazy stunts. The sillier they acted, the more people laughed.

In one movie, the Marx Brothers decided to take a boat trip. They got a very tiny cabin which was soon filled with people and luggage. Soon there was no room, but people kept coming in. Finally, someone opened the cabin door and everyone tumbled out onto the floor.

The Marx Brothers really were brothers. They began performing when they were still children. Their other brothers, Zeppo and Gummo, also appeared with them for awhile.

Some of the Marx Brothers films are "Animal Crackers", "Duck Soup" and "A Night at the Opera". All of their films were made in the 1930's and 1940's. But children and adults still enjoy the Marx Brothers films today.

1. **The main idea of this story is:**
   a. The Marx Brothers took a trip.
   b. The Marx Brothers made people laugh.
   c. The Marx Brothers spoke Italian.

2. **The Marx Brothers:**
   a. made movies a long time ago
   b. were singing stars
   c. only made sad movies

3. **How many Marx Brothers were there?**
   a. 2
   b. 8
   c. 5

4. **What does <u>chomped</u> mean?**
   a. chewed
   b. swallowed
   c. jumped

5. **People thought the Marx Brothers were very funny because:**
   a. They wore funny clothes and acted silly.
   b. They were brothers.
   c. They never worked alone.

     FS-32046 Reading

The "Say Hey" Kid

Willie Mays was born to play baseball. His first toy was a baseball. He was given his first baseball glove when he was three years old. His father, grandfather, and uncle had all been baseball players. They began teaching Willie to play baseball when he was only six years old.

Willie joined the New York Giants when he was 20. He was good at everything he did in baseball. He was a great hitter. He won the batting championship in 1954. He also stole more than 300 bases. Willie could catch almost any ball that was hit into the outfield. Some of the catches he made seemed impossible to do.

Willie Mays was loved by sports fans. They called him the "Say Hey" kid because he could never remember anyone's name. He called everyone "Say Hey".

In 1973, Willie Mays left baseball at the age of 42. He had hit 660 home runs and had played almost 3,000 games.

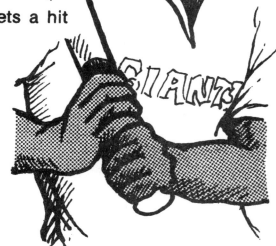

1. **The main idea of this story is:**
   a. Willie Mays was a champion baseball player.
   b. Willie Mays liked to play football.
   c. Willie Mays lived in New York.

2. **The New York Giants:**
   a. were very tall
   b. ate too much
   c. are a baseball team

3. **To** <u>**steal bases**</u> **means:**
   a. carry the bases away
   b. run the bases before the next batter up gets a hit
   c. hide under the base

4. **Willie was called the "Say Hey" kid because:**
   a. He liked to talk a lot.
   b. He liked to eat hay.
   c. He could never remember anyone's name.

5. **Willie Mays probably left baseball because:**
   a. He didn't like baseball anymore.
   b. He wanted to be a teacher.
   c. He was getting too old to play well.

Name _____ Date _____

Read each paragraph. Decide which answer best tells the <u>main idea</u> and circle it.

1. The Komodo Dragon is actually a lizard. It can grow to be 10 feet long and is the largest lizard living today. The Komodo is called a dragon because it looks like one—long tail, sharp teeth and scaly skin.

   a. how long dragons grow   b. another name for lizards   c. what Komodos look like

2. A **phobia** is something you are afraid of. You might have a fear of cats or spiders or a fear of being in crowds. But here is a phobia to end all phobias: **arachibutyrophobia!** It is the fear of getting peanut butter stuck in the roof of your mouth.

   a. where peanut butter sticks
   b. fears called phobias
   c. a phobia about cats

3. Do you have a lot of insects wandering around the house? If so, a toad would make a great pet. Toads eat only foods that move—bugs, flies, beetles and other pests. Toads get very hungry in the summer. It takes 10,000 insects to fill up their stomachs. So don't swat any flies! Your toad might croak!

   a. how many flies toads eat   b. what toads like to eat   c. a good house pet

4. Once there was a man named John. He lived in England in a town called Sandwich. John loved to play cards. He never wanted to leave the card table, not even for meals. One day, John came up with a brilliant idea: "Why not just put some meat between two pieces of bread? Then I can play cards and eat at the same time." Today John's invention is known as the sandwich.

   a. a brilliant invention
   b. the man who invented bread
   c. eating at a card table

──────── **Thinking Time** ────────

Read the next two questions carefully. Answer them on the back of this paper.

1. People are terribly afraid of many different things. How do you think someone might have developed a fear of water?

2. Finish this sentence in your own words: John eats a sandwich and plays cards at the same time. I eat a sandwich and _____.

Name _____ **Date** _____

Read each paragraph. Decide which answer best tells the <u>main idea</u> and circle it.

1. One of the shortest human beings ever to have lived was a girl named Lucia Zarata. At age 17, Lucia measured one foot, eight inches tall. She weighed only a little over four pounds. That is smaller than most babies when they are born.

   a. the shortest man in history   b. a very short girl   c. how much babies weigh

2. The color of a room can affect the way you feel. Blue or gray may make you feel sad. Yellow and white are cheery colors. Peach is the best color of all, though. This color makes you feel relaxed and comfortable.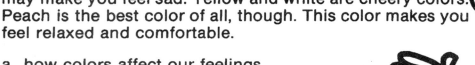

   a. how colors affect our feelings
   b. having a feel for color
   c. the best color for feeling cheery

3. I was going to take my first trip on a jet. I was so excited when the day finally came. "Well, our luggage is all checked in," Dad said. "Let's go up to the boarding gate. Our plane leaves in 20 minutes."

   a. a funny father   b. a ruined trip   c. my first plane trip

4. Martha knows every elephant joke on this whole earth! This is the newest one she told me yesterday: "Why did the elephant stand on the marshmallow?" Naturally, I didn't know. "Because he didn't want to fall in the hot chocolate," Martha chuckled. I think Martha made that one up all by herself.

   a. a girl who likes elephants
   b. a girl who tells elephant jokes
   c. elephants that tell jokes

——— Thinking Time ———

Read the next two questions carefully. Answer them on the back of this paper.

1. Read story #1. What things do you do by yourself that Lucia would have trouble doing?

2. Tell how each of these colors might make you feel: red, purple, black, brown, and orange.

Name _____ **Date** _____

Read each paragraph. Decide which answer best tells the <u>main idea</u> and circle it.

1. Once a man lost the tip of his nose in a fight. He had a new tip made out of gold. The man polished his nose all the time. It really shined! He was very proud of it. He did have trouble blowing his gold nose, though.

   a. having a fight   b. how to make a gold nose   c. a new nose

2. Why wasn't the New World named after Christopher Columbus? Until the day he died, Columbus insisted that he had discovered an unexplored area of Asia. If Columbus had known his geography better, we might be called Columbians and not Americans today.

   a. the naming of the New World
   b. who really discovered America
   c. exploring land in Asia

3. The Amazon River in South America is the biggest river in the world. It is not a very friendly river. The water is full of snakes, alligators and many deadly kinds of fish. You probably wouldn't want to swim in the Amazon.

   a. the biggest river   b. river of no return   c. swimming with snakes

4. One day I met someone at a party. I couldn't think of a **single** thing to say to her. Suddenly, I remembered something fascinating. "Do you know what kind of transportation is most widely used in the U.S.?" I asked. "It's not the car. It's the elevator! Elevators travel more than 1.5 billion miles a year." All she said was "Oh" and walked away.

   a. the fastest car in the U.S.
   b. making conversation
   c. telling stories in an elevator

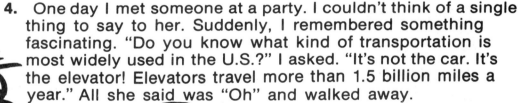

─Thinking Time─

Read the next two questions carefully. Answer them on the back of this paper.

1. Read story #2. What would have happened if a man named Stillwell had discovered America?

2. We travel by car. Name four other things in which you can travel.

73

Name _____ **Date** _____

Read each paragraph. Decide which answer best tells the <u>main idea</u> and circle it.

1. This is something that will bring you good luck: put a corn cob behind your ear. Be sure to eat the corn first, though.

   a. wishing for corn   b. a good luck charm   c. how corn grows

2. The cheetah is the fastest land animal on earth. This cat can sprint up to 70 miles an hour! Imagine a cheetah running alongside your car while you are driving down the highway! Both of you would get a ticket for going over the speed limit.

   a. running 70 miles per hour
   b. the fastest animal
   c. speeding on the highway

3. Once there were two painters, Gus and Georgy, working on a house. Georgy was on the ladder and Gus was mixing paints below. "Have you got a tight grip on that paint brush?" Gus called up to Georgy.
   Georgy answered, "Yes sire-e-e."
   "Good!" Gus said. "Hang on 'cause I need the ladder." Gus took the ladder away.

   a. painting a house   b. using a paint brush   c. a surprised painter

4. Long ago, people lit their Christmas trees by fastening real candles on the branches. Many trees with these decorations burned down. Then someone suggested using electric lights instead. These white lights were not very popular at first. But when they were painted red, blue and green, everyone started using electric lights on their trees.

   a. lighting up Christmas trees
   b. why candles are dangerous
   c. how electric lights first became popular

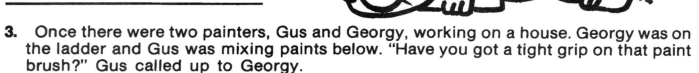

────────────Thinking Time────────────

Read the next two questions carefully. Answer them on the back of this paper.

1. Corn is supposed to bring good luck. Name two other kinds of good luck charms you know about.

2. Read story #3. Draw a picture to show the expression on Georgy's face when Gus took the ladder.

74

Read each paragraph. Decide which answer best tells the <u>main idea</u> and circle it.

1. Not long ago, there lived a man who never slept a day in his life. Doctors watched him day and night for months. He never took so much as a cat nap! Only once did this man sleep—on the day he died at age 94!

    a. sleeping for 94 years   b. how to live without sleep   c. a man who never slept

2. Thousands of years ago, people had only one name—Gregory, for example. When someone talked about Gregory, they would say, "Gregory of Albans is coming to see me." This was very simple—until too many Gregorys were born in Albans. Read the next story to find out what happened.

    a. where Gregorys are born
    b. how people were named
    c. how many names people had

3. Your last name is your **surname**. Let's say your name is Anthony. Your father's name is John. Your full name would be Anthony Johnson (son-of-John). This was just one of many ways used to make surnames. Today, everyone has at least two names. Some people have seven or eight names.

    a. how surnames are made   b. what Johnson means   c. when surnames are used

4. Here is a story about a very unusual prison. It is not much different from other prisons—except for one thing. If a prisoner escapes, the guard on duty is in real trouble! He must serve the rest of the sentence of the escaped prisoner. One time a prisoner had 99 years left on his sentence when he escaped. He was never captured.

    a. sentences that are too long
    b. a different kind of prison
    c. prisoners who are guards

──────────────── **Thinking Time** ────────────────

Read the next two questions carefully. Answer them on the back of this paper.

1. What does the saying "take a cat nap" mean?

2. Write a good title: Many people have nicknames like Bugsy, Duke, Bunny and Lovey Dovey. I have a friend named Poppsy. Everyone knows who I'm talking about even if I don't say her last name.

Name _____ Date _____

Read each paragraph. Decide which answer best tells the <u>main idea</u> and circle it.

1. Banana riddles are some of the funniest of all. How do you like this one: What is orange, goes click-click and is good for your eyes? ANSWER: a ball point carrot.

   a. what pens look like   b. a ridiculous riddle   c. orange bananas

_____

2. The first piece of bubble gum was named Blibber-Blubber. You could blow huge bubbles with it. There was just one problem with this gum. If it popped, it made a terrible mess. Sometimes it might take three days to peel it off your face.

   a. how to blow huge bubbles
   b. the first bubble gum
   c. some problems with bubble gum

_____

3. When winter comes, some snakes coil up and go to sleep. The colder the weather gets, the colder the snake gets. Its body is so stiff, the snake can't move at all. These snakes can be stuck like this for a very long time. They must wait for the warm weather to return. Then they can uncoil again.

   a. where snakes coil   b. snakes in cold weather   c. getting stiff in winter

_____

4. Crash! Another bottle of milk dropped on the floor. John Van Wormer looked at the mess. "I'm going to do something about this!" he said. John went to work making a paper milk bottle. He made one easily, but it was slow going after that. Americans didn't want to give up their glass bottles. It was 20 years before paper cartons were finally accepted.

   a. making bottles that won't break
   b. changing glass into paper
   c. crying over spilt milk

─────────── **Thinking Time** ───────────

Read the next two questions carefully. Answer them on the back of this paper.

1. Think of a good title for this story: Meals can be fixed very fast today. Open a can, tear open a bag, pop a top and dinner is ready!

2. Write three words to describe how a snake: Moves _____ ; Looks _____ ; Sounds _____ .

Read each paragraph. Decide which answer best tells the <u>main idea</u> and circle it.

1. In the early 1800's, schools were called "blab schools". That's because everyone blabbed! The whole class said their lessons out loud—all at the same time.

    a. what schools were called   b. lessons in blabbing   c. blabbing out loud

2. Dip. Write. Dip. Write. Into the ink bottle, back to the paper. Writing with a fountain pen took a long time. It could be very messy, too. And at school, boys liked to dip girls' pigtails into the ink bottles. Why couldn't there be a pen with the ink already in it? Someone did finally invent the ball point pen. Now everyone just "clicks and writes". Today, fountain pens are mainly a decoration on a desk.

    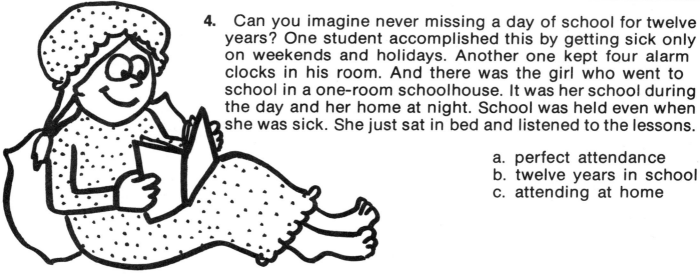

    a. the end of ink bottles
    b. a new way to write with ink
    c. where fountain pens are found

3. The largest bird in the world is the ostrich. It is eight feet tall and weighs more than 300 pounds. The ostrich can't fly, but it really doesn't need to. At full speed it can run 50 miles an hour.

    a. an unusual bird   b. world's largest bird   c. why ostriches can't fly

4. Can you imagine never missing a day of school for twelve years? One student accomplished this by getting sick only on weekends and holidays. Another one kept four alarm clocks in his room. And there was the girl who went to school in a one-room schoolhouse. It was her school during the day and her home at night. School was held even when she was sick. She just sat in bed and listened to the lessons.

    a. perfect attendance
    b. twelve years in school
    c. attending at home

——————— **Thinking Time** ———————

Read the next two questions carefully. Answer them on the back of this paper.

1. The potato chip and french fries were invented by a cook 100 years ago. How do you think they came to be invented?

2. If you have "set a record" what have you done?

Read each paragraph. Decide which answer best tells the <u>main idea</u> and circle it.

1. As we get older, our sense of smell gets old, too. The nose seems to give out faster than any of the other sense organs. That's probably a good thing, especially if you live near a garbage dump.

   a. the smell of garbage   b. when noses get old   c. sensing a smell

2. Do you have a sore throat? Get a piece of raw meat and put some pepper on it. Wrap it around your neck for a few days. This is what people did 100 years ago. When the meat turned rotten, the sore throat got better (or you got even sicker from the smell).

   a. how meat makes you sick
   b. why throats are sore
   c. a cure for sore throats

3. The earliest kind of shoe we know about is the sandal. The second type of shoe to come along was the boot. It was worn mainly for traveling. Then about 500 years ago, shoes with very long points became popular. They looked ridiculous! The points were so-o-o-o long, they had to be tied at the knees. Can you imagine skateboarding in these shoes?

   a. how pointed shoes looked   b. different kinds of shoes   c. the most popular shoes

4. About 70 years ago, a woman named Josephine was a new bride in a new house. She could not seem to get through the day without cutting herself. Her husband decided to take action. He couldn't take everything sharp out of the house. So instead, he cut up strips of tape. A piece of cotton was stuck in the middle of each strip. He left the strips all over the house for Josephine. Do you know what these strips of tape are called today?

   a. how husbands can be helpful
   b. invention of the bandage
   c. a very clumsy bride

───────────── **Thinking Time** ─────────────

Read the next two questions carefully. Answer them on the back of this paper.

1. Think of a good title for this story: Your mouth can make sounds, hum a tune, play the trumpet and blow bubbles.

2. Name five different activities for which you need to buy five different kinds of shoes.

 FS-32046 Reading

Name _____ **Date** _____

Read each paragraph. Decide which answer best tells the <u>main idea</u> and circle it.

1. There are some green sheep wandering around England. They have lawns growing on their backs! How could this be? Someone must have dropped grass seeds onto their wool. With all the sun and rain, the seeds grew. The sheep don't seem to mind. But what if someone decides to mow the lawn?

   a. growing grass seeds   b. greenback sheep   c. little grass sheep

2. Long ago, people guessed what time it was by looking at the sun. Later "shadow sticks" were set in the ground. When the shadow was the shortest, it was noontime. From the shadow stick came the sundial. It is one of the oldest known instruments for telling time. Other early time-telling instruments were the hourglass and the water clock.

   a. how shadow sticks tell time
   b. early ways to tell time
   c. telling time by the sun

3. You have probably heard of artists who paint in very unusual ways. Some people put brushes between their toes or their teeth and draw. One of the most remarkable artists ever to live was a man named Huang Erh-nan. He painted butterflies and flowers, but not with his teeth or toes. Huang used his tongue as a brush. He even kept the ink for drawing his pictures in a corner of his mouth.

   a. an unusual way to paint   b. turning tongues into brushes   c. an artist with toes

4. The youngest girl ever to win an Olympic gold medal was Marjorie Gesring. She won her medal in 1936 in a diving event. At the time, Marjorie was only 13 years and nine months old.

   a. the youngest Olympic diver
   b. the youngest medal winner
   c. winning at the Olympics

──────── **Thinking Time** ────────

Read the next two questions carefully. Answer them on the back of this paper.

1. Finish the sentence. Years ago people told time by sundials. But they could only tell time when _____

2. Ben is a champion skateboarder. He has won many contests. He would like to be in the Olympics. Why can't he?

Read each paragraph. Decide which answer best tells the <u>main idea</u> and circle it.

1. There are a lot of different sayings about noses: The horse won by a nose. She's got a nose for news. He hit it right on the nose! Do you know what these sayings mean?

   a. how horses win races   b. learning sayings   c. sayings about noses

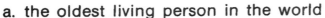

2. A tree in California known as "General Sherman" is one of the oldest living things in the world. This giant sequoia is 272 feet tall and still growing. Scientists think the tree was "born" at least 3,000 to 4,000 years ago. That's really living to a ripe old age.

   a. the oldest living person in the world
   b. who General Sherman was
   c. the oldest living sequoia

3. About one million earthquakes occur every year around the world. Of these, 6000 are strong enough to be felt by humans. There have been some terrible earthquakes on land. But some of the most violent earthquakes have occurred at sea far from cities and towns.

   a. when earthquakes occur   b. facts about earthquakes   c. earthquakes in one year

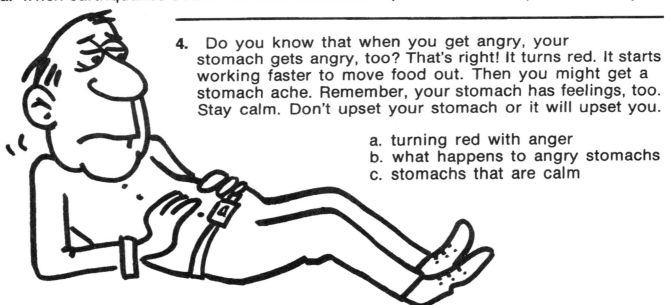

4. Do you know that when you get angry, your stomach gets angry, too? That's right! It turns red. It starts working faster to move food out. Then you might get a stomach ache. Remember, your stomach has feelings, too. Stay calm. Don't upset your stomach or it will upset you.

   a. turning red with anger
   b. what happens to angry stomachs
   c. stomachs that are calm

———— Thinking Time ————

Read the next two questions carefully. Answer them on the back of this paper.

1. Write the main idea of this story. The saying "Terry got cold feet" doesn't mean her feet were cold. It means she was afraid to do something.

2. Read story #4. How does a stomach sometimes act like a person?

Name _____   **Date** _____

Read each paragraph. Decide which answer best tells the <u>main idea</u> and circle it.

1. Do you know how policemen came to be called "cops"? Years ago, policemen wore badges that were made of copper. People started calling policemen "coppers". Later on, the name was shortened to "cops".

    a. names for policemen   b. what copper is   c. how "cops" got started

2. One of the most useful, time-saving inventions of all time is the photocopier. Years ago, it could take days to get even one page reprinted! Today, a page can be copied in five seconds, a whole book in less than an hour! The photocopier is an amazing machine.

    a. time-saving inventions
    b. machines that make copies
    c. a remarkable invention

3. Once there was a cowboy named Lou.
    Who had a white horse called Fazoo.
    One day while visiting the town of Poofair,
    Fazoo spied a pretty, brown-spotted mare,
    So Fazoo told Lou: "Toodle-oo".

    a. how Lou lost his horse   b. words that rhyme   c. horses that can talk

4. Surfing first came to the United States around 1910. But it took 50 years before it really became popular. This was one sport that got off to a bad start! In the summer of 1958, groups of surfers "took over" some beaches. Swimmers complained loudly, "Those weirdos on ironing boards! They're dangerous! Send them to the North Pole to surf!" It took a few years but swimmers and surfers finally worked out their problems.

    a. the early days of surfing
    b. why surfing is dangerous
    c. why swimmers get angry

———— **Thinking Time** ————

Read the next two questions carefully. Answer them on the back of this paper.

1. What would policemen be called if their badges were made of steel or their shoes made of rubber? Use your imagination.

2. Surfing is a water sport. Name two other sports you can do only in the water.

81   FS-32046 Reading

Read each paragraph. Decide which answer best tells the <u>main idea</u> and circle it.

1. The word dinosaur means "terrible lizard". Some dinosaurs weren't very terrible, though. They were small, about the size of a chicken. Others were no bigger than a man. They had long bodies. Their hands and feet looked like a rooster's.

   a. what dinosaur means b. where dinosaurs lived c. how some dinosaurs appeared

2. Hummingbirds are the only birds that can fly backwards. They can also fly in one place—almost like a helicopter.

   a. two unusual things about hummingbirds
   b. birds that look like helicopters
   c. why hummingbirds hum

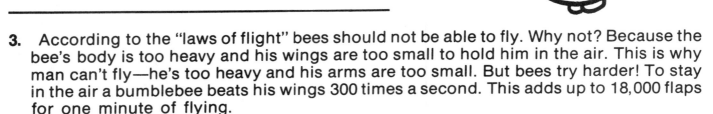

3. According to the "laws of flight" bees should not be able to fly. Why not? Because the bee's body is too heavy and his wings are too small to hold him in the air. This is why man can't fly—he's too heavy and his arms are too small. But bees try harder! To stay in the air a bumblebee beats his wings 300 times a second. This adds up to 18,000 flaps for one minute of flying.

   a. why bees can't fly   b. why man can't fly   c. breaking the laws of flight

4. The highest mountain in the world is Mount Everest on the continent of Asia. You have to be an expert mountain climber to make the trip up this mountain. It is a very dangerous hike. One missed step and you could fall 29,028 feet straight down.

   a. climbing Mount Everest
   b. the world's tallest mountain
   c. a dangerous mountain fall

———————— **Thinking Time** ————————

Read the next two questions carefully. Answer them on the back of this paper.

1. Write the main idea of this sentence: Some dinosaurs were only eight feet long, but other dinosaurs grew to be 70 or 80 feet long.

2. Do you know what makes bees buzz and hummingbirds hum?

Read each paragraph. Decide which answer best tells the <u>main idea</u> and circle it.

1. Has your teacher ever said, "Learn these words by heart?" Centuries ago, people thought the heart, not the brain, was the center of learning. All ideas came from the heart. Now you know how the expression "learn by heart" got started.

   a. where ideas begin   b. learning by heart   c. how one expression got started

_____

2. Do you know why boxer dogs are called boxers? When this dog gets excited, he will sit up on his hind legs. His front paws make punching motions just like a boxer.

   a. what makes boxers box
   b. how boxers got their names
   c. how boxing got started

3. Do you want to know an easy way to spell "arithmetic"? Just say these words to yourself one by one: a rat in the house might eat that ice cream. Write down the first letter of each word as you say it. You will have spelled "arithmetic" (if you said every word in the saying, that is).

   a. rats like ice cream   b. learning arithmetic sayings   c. a fun way to spell

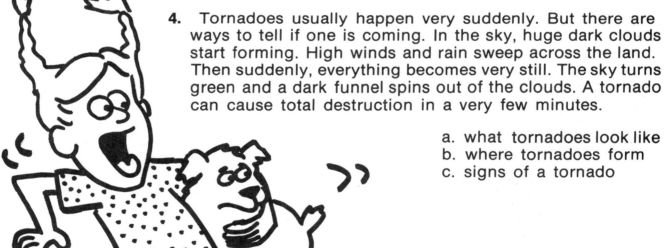

4. Tornadoes usually happen very suddenly. But there are ways to tell if one is coming. In the sky, huge dark clouds start forming. High winds and rain sweep across the land. Then suddenly, everything becomes very still. The sky turns green and a dark funnel spins out of the clouds. A tornado can cause total destruction in a very few minutes.

   a. what tornadoes look like
   b. where tornadoes form
   c. signs of a tornado

_____ **Thinking Time** _____

Read the next two questions carefully. Answer them on the back of this paper.

1. Look at #3. Now write F-U-N-N-Y. Make up words to go with each letter in funny. Your saying will help you to remember how to spell funny.

2. What might happen if you left your bike outside and a tornado hit?

83

Name _____ Date _____

Read each paragraph. Decide which answer best tells the <u>main idea</u> and circle it.

1. Here is a good way to start off the morning. Get out of bed on the right side. Put your right foot on the floor first. If you forget to do this, walk on your hands back to bed. Then start over again.

    a. stepping on the floor
    b. starting off the day
    c. making the right move

    _____

2. Thousands of years ago, the symbol for the letter "K" was a hand with the fingers curved. The Egyptians called the letter "kaph" which means "palm of the hand". In 600 B.C. the Greeks put the letter in their alphabet. They made the "K" in the form we still use today.

    a. how the "K" developed
    b. what "K" means
    c. a symbol for a letter

    _____

3. Elephants are very nearsighted animals. They cannot see anything clearly unless it is close to them. Because of this hunters can easily capture elephants. The Asian elephant is easily trained to work. It learns to understand its master's tone of voice when given directions. If treated well, the elephant seems to be very happy as a work animal.

    a. why elephants can't see hunters
    b. interesting facts about elephants
    c. how elephants are captured

4. The oldest letter in the alphabet is the "O". Its sound and shape has been the same for thousands of years. About 300 years ago, the "J" and the "U" were added to the alphabet. I wonder how John and Utah were spelled before then?

    a. the sounds of letters
    b. facts about some letters
    c. the newest alphabet

———————————— **Thinking Time** ————————————

Read the next two questions carefully. Answer them on the back of this paper.

1. What does the saying "to get off on the right foot" mean?

2. Fill in this sentence: Elephants can't see things that are _____ .
   Something has to _____ for an elephant to see it.

84   FS-32046 Reading

Name _____ Date _____

Read each paragraph. Decide which answer best tells the <u>main idea</u> and circle it.

1. The Australian walking fish leads a double life. This fish can not only swim but walk, too. His fins become "feet" on land. He can climb low-hanging tree branches, lie back and sunbathe for a few hours or more.

   a. a fish that only swims   b. fins that are feet   c. a water and land fish

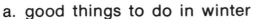

2. The time to read a new book or learn 30 spelling words is during the wintertime. When it's very cold your brain works better and faster. So if you ever wanted to learn all about MICROPALEONTOLOGY, winter is the time to start.

   a. good things to do in winter
   b. how fast the brain works
   c. when brains work the best

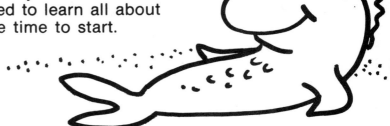

3. Roller skates were first made by a man named Joseph. He was a musician, but he loved to invent, too. One night, Joseph was invited to play music at a ball. He rang the doorbell. He then rolled across the dance floor on his skates, playing his violin. Only one thing went wrong. Joseph couldn't stop. He crashed into a mirror. Joseph wasn't invited to play his violin at a ball again.

   a. a famous musican   b. the first roller skates   c. skating at a ball

4. Let's go to a store that sells 31 flavors of ice cream. You want to get every possible double-dip combination they have—one each day. Do you know how many times you would have to go into the store? 496 times! That's more than a year of daily ice-cream-eating.

   a. drippy ice cream
   b. eating ice cream every day
   c. 496 ice cream stores

──────────── **Thinking Time** ────────────

Read the next two questions carefully. Answer them on the back of this paper.

1. If your brain works slower in hot weather, what two things would you not like to do when it is 100 degrees?

2. Look around your classroom. Many things in the room were invented to make life easier. List as many of these things as you can.

Read each paragraph. Decide which answer best tells the <u>main idea</u> and circle it.

1.   Here's a little brain-tickler for you to work out. Tom gave Millie two coins. Together they equaled 30 cents. But one of them wasn't a quarter. How did Tom do this? (Answer: The one that wasn't a quarter was a nickel--ha, ha, tee, hee).

   a. solving a brain tickler b. 30 cents in coins c. tickling brains with money

2.   There is a lake in Massachusetts named Chargogagogmancaugagogchaubunagungamaug. It was named by two tribes of Indians living along the shores of a lake. The name is supposed to mean: "You fish on your side, we fish on our side, and nobody fishes in the middle."

   a. a lake with an unusual name
   b. how a lake gets its name
   c. where Indians can fish

3.   Hundreds of years ago, huge amounts of gold were found in the mountains of Peru. The Inca Indians used some of this gold in a strange way. Little pieces of gold were shined and polished. Then they were ground into the Indians' front teeth. If one of them smiled, the sparkle would just about blind you!

   a. where gold teeth are found b. an unusual Indian custom c. polished teeth

4.   "Ah, yes! This bump on your head tells me something very important. You should be a wagon master. That is the perfect job for you!" In the old west, some men went to see future-tellers when they wanted to know what kind of job to get. The future-tellers rubbed their fingers all over the man's head. He felt all the bumps and valleys. Somehow (no one knows quite how, though) the future-teller would know exactly what job the man should get.

   a. how to find a job
   b. how future-tellers told the future
   c. what bumps and valleys mean

──────Thinking Time──────

Read the next two questions carefully. Then answer them on the back of this paper.

1. Your are going to search for gold. Make a list of these things:

   WHAT TO WEAR   SUPPLIES TO TAKE

2. Write the main idea of this story: Tim wants to be a fireman. He will study hard and exercise every day. Firemen have to be strong.

Read each paragraph. Decide which answer best tells the <u>main idea</u> and circle it.

1. Here's a riddle for you to figure out: What coat has no sleeves, no buttons, no front and fits best when put on wet? (Hint: the answer rhymes with "faint").

   a. finding rhyming words   b. solving a riddle   c. rhyming riddle

2. Fifty million years from now, Earth won't look anything like it does today. Scientists think that Los Angeles will be an island in the ocean. Big chunks of Africa will also break off and float away. And the Hawaiian Islands will just keep drifting further and further north.

   a. Earth in 50 million years
   b. when Earth will disappear
   c. where islands drift

3. Black Bart was one of the most famous stagecoach robbers of the old west. But "Blackie" was not your everyday robber. He carried out his robberies with perfect manners. Never once did he forget to say "please" or "thank you" as he robbed the passengers of all their belongings. Black Bart was a poet, too, although not a good one. He would make up a poem to read at the end of each hold-up, then ride off into the sunset.

   a. a poet named Black Bart   b. a gentleman robber   c. a famous stage coach

4. Most people write their names the same way day after day, year after year. President John F. Kennedy was not one of these people. It seems Kennedy never signed his name the same way twice. Sometimes his autographs were impossible to read. Only an expert on Kennedy handwriting could tell if it was the "real thing".

   a. learning to read autographs
   b. the way Kennedy signed his name
   c. how Kennedy's name looked twice

──────── **Thinking Time** ────────

Read the next two questions carefully. Answer them on the back of this paper.

1. Los Angeles will be an island in 50 million years. Describe what an island is like.

2. Name two reasons why a stagecoach would not be comfortable to ride in while traveling.

87

Name _____ **Date** _____

Read each paragraph. Decide which answer best tells the <u>main idea</u> and circle it.

1. Bread is one of the most popular foods in the world. Without bread there wouldn't be any sandwiches. Or hamburgers. Or hot dogs. Or pizza. Terrible thought! Think about it. Hardly a day goes by without most of us eating bread!

    a. how to fix a sandwich   b. the many uses of bread   c. the bread of life

---

2.

    A man had a nose that looked like a pickle.
    A bee came along and started to tickle.
    This isn't very funny,
    I don't have any honey.
    Said the bee, "I'm thirsty and my tongue needs a lick-le".

    a. a pickle for a nose
    b. a very silly poem
    c. a honey pickle

---

3. Levi's are called Levi's because a man named Levi invented them. Levi Strauss lived in gold country. Gold mining was hard work. Miners' pants wore out very fast. Levi decided to make pants out of a cloth called canvas. It was very strong. Soon all the miners started asking for a pair of "that man Levi's" pants. Today, Levi's are worn all over the world—and not just by miners!

    a. how Levi made Levi's   b. how Levi's came to be invented   c. why Levis are better

4. Here is a brain-teaser for you to try: a) eight thousand, b) eight hundred and c) 88 dollars is written $8,888. How would you write twelve thousand, twelve hundred and twelve dollars? (Hint: add a, b and c and see what you get. Then do the same thing for the next one.)

    a. a teasing problem
    b. learning to add
    c. tickling your brain

----------------------- **Thinking Time** -----------------------

Read the next two questions carefully. Answer them on the back of this paper.

1. Think of your favorite foods. Draw a sandwich with these foods in it. Write down what you put in your sandwich.

2. Levi's are strong pants. Name three kinds of jobs where people always wear Levis. They need pants that won't tear easily.

Name _____ **Date** _____

Read each paragraph. Decide which answer best tells the <u>main idea</u> and circle it.

1.   Eighty years ago, the volcano Krakatoa exploded. Almost the whole island was blown away. When the explosion ended, a search party went to the island. They found nothing alive. Nothing—except a tiny spider spinning its web under a rock.

    a. the end of an island b. how Krakatoa exploded c. searching for volcanoes

---

2.   Do you know what letter in the alphabet is used most often? Far and away, it is the "E". And (just in case someone asks you sometime) more words start with "S" than any other letter.

    a. how many times "S" is used
    b. alphabet letters used most often
    c. how many words start with "E"

---

3.   Millions of years ago, there was a **reptile** called Dimetrodon. It had a big fin down its back. This fin has always been a mystery. Fins usually help fish swim. Yet the Dimetrodons weren't water animals. No one has yet discovered any use for the Dimetrodon's fin.

    a. fish with fins b. a mysterious fin c. reptiles called Dimetrodons

---

4.   When you are hunting alligators, sneak up on them while their jaws are closed. An alligator's strong jaw can crush cattle bones. But when its jaws are shut, you can hold them closed with your bare hands! This way, you can capture an alligator without using a weapon.

    a. when to catch an alligator
    b. jaws that crush bones
    c. swamp creature

━━━━ Thinking Time ━━━━

Read the next two questions carefully. Answer them on the back of this paper.

1. If something is a "mystery" what does it mean?

2. Write the main idea of this sentence: Alligators have sharp teeth, are gray or green in color and have skin that is tough.

             FS-32046 Reading

1. The main idea of this story is:
   a. People go to jail.
   b. Don't tell secrets.
   c. Don't talk to boys.

2. Maria's friends all said they would:
   a. keep her secret
   b. call the police
   c. tell the teacher

3. Why did Maria's father get a ticket?
   a. He went too fast.
   b. He went backwards.
   c. His car only had two wheels.

4. A <u>ticket</u> in this story is:
   a. what you need to get into the movies
   b. what you get when you break the law
   c. something you get at the circus

5. The story doesn't say, but Maria will probably:
   a. go home and watch TV
   b. get a new father
   c. be sorry she told her secret

90   FS-32046 Reading

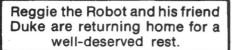

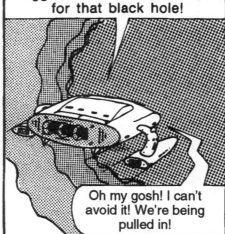

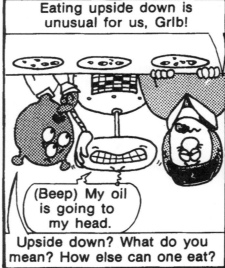

1. **The main idea of this story is:**
   a. Eating upside down makes you sick.
   b. Robots can talk.
   c. Reggie and Duke have lots of adventures.

2. **From Grlb's planet, Earth was:**
   a. very, very far away
   b. just around the corner
   c. square

3. **Reggie and Duke entered a:**
   a. candy shop
   b. park
   c. black hole

4. **Universe means:**
   a. a kind of poetry
   b. everything and everyone in space
   c. a kind of school

5. **Reggie and Duke were probably:**
   a. glad that someone helped them
   b. in a bad mood
   c. wishing they could live on Xzlpkgsytn

                   FS-32046 Reading

It was a dark and stormy night—

What a night! It's raining cats and dogs! I took the wrong turn back there. Maybe the people in this house can help me.

Hello! Anyone home? I hear music but the house seems deserted.

I don't like the looks of this. Maybe someone is upstairs.

Hi! Come join us.

Help! Somebody save me! / What's the matter with him?

It's midnight, folks! Take off your masks.

BONG BONG

That mask was hot.

I love costume parties!

1. The main idea of this story is:
- a. Stay out of the rain.
- b. Wear a raincoat.
- c. Things aren't always as they seem.

2. The man in this story:
- a. thought he saw real monsters
- b. liked costume parties
- c. was not scared

3. The man needed:
- a. a Frankenstein mask
- b. directions
- c. a sandwich

4. Raining cats and dogs means:
- a. Cats and dogs are coming out of the sky.
- b. Cats and dogs are fighting.
- c. It's raining very hard.

5. You can tell from the story that:
- a. The people at the party were having fun.
- b. No one wore a costume.
- c. There were lots of Draculas.

* On the back of this paper, draw yourself in a costume you'd wear to a party.

1. **The main idea of this story is:**
   a. Who is really in the zoo?
   b. People like to dance.
   c. Monkeys are cute.

2. **The apes thought the dancers were:**
   a. small
   b. boring
   c. funny

3. **The apes wanted to give the dancers:**
   a. pizza
   b. popcorn
   c. peanuts

4. **In this story, the word <u>beat</u> means:**
   a. to hit someone
   b. the rhythm of a song
   c. cleaning a rug

5. **You can tell from the story that apes like to:**
   a. dance
   b. eat hamburgers
   c. watch people

* On the back of this paper, write a different ending to this story.

1. **The main idea of this story is:**
    a. Always look through the garbage.
    b. You don't always get what you wish for.
    c. Give your mother presents.
2. **The genie was:**
    a. glad to get away from George
    b. green and blue
    c. George's uncle
3. **Instead of "no more school" George got:**
    a. a drink that was cool
    b. a kiddie pool
    c. a set of tools
4. **A genie is:**
    a. a very smart person
    b. a tiny elf
    c. a spirit that does what you want
5. **It doesn't say, but George probably:**
    a. wouldn't trust genies again
    b. would like his rubber duck
    c. would look through lots more garbage cans

* On the back of this paper, write three wishes you'd want the genie to grant you.

FS-32046 Reading

Sam! Did you do the science homework? I was too busy watching TV. Did you see "The Monster that Ate New Jersey"?

No, I missed it. But I did part of the homework. I just wrote down the answers. You can borrow it.

Michelle! Can I borrow the math homework? I was too busy to do it.

DUE TODAY:
SCIENCE
MATH
SOCIAL STUDIES

Boy, Steve! You never do your homework. This is the last time!

Can you believe that guy Steve? He borrowed homework for every subject from all his friends! He'll get in trouble one of these days.

TEE HEE!

I know. He needs a good lesson.

Let's see. Social studies, science and math after lunch. This is Sam's science. Michelle's math. No, wait. This is getting all mixed up. Ooops, the teacher!

GULP!

All right, class. Please give the answers when I call your name.

Steve, why did the Pilgrims leave England?

Uh, uh, because of oxygen.

What? Where did they land?

In a crater on the moon! I mean 1492! 3×12=48! Oh, no!

I'm so embarrassed. I wish they'd make a movie called "The Monster that Ate Steve"!

USC

1. **The main idea of this story is:**
   a. Science is hard.
   b. Teachers are mean.
   c. Do your own homework.
2. **Steve's friends:**
   a. were angry with him
   b. liked doing Steve's homework for him
   c. weren't at school
3. **Steve was busy:**
   a. doing homework
   b. playing football
   c. watching TV

4. **A <u>crater</u> on the moon is:**
   a. a big piece of cheese
   b. a big hole on the moon
   c. a spaceship
5. **Steve seemed to feel:**
   a. happy
   b. ashamed
   c. hungry

* On the back of this paper, write three different titles for this story.

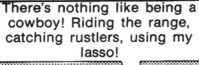

1. The main idea of this story is:
   a. Jeff has a good imagination.
   b. Being a cowboy is boring.
   c. Horses aren't real.

2. Jeff helps catch:
   a. the sheriff
   b. the thieves
   c. some fish

3. Jeff's horse is named:
   a. Rover
   b. Silver
   c. Black Beauty

4. A <u>sheriff</u> is:
   a. a kind of policeman
   b. a kind of car
   c. a vegetable kids like

5. Jeff probably:
   a. doesn't like horses
   b. will go riding again
   c. is very old

* On the back of this paper, draw another adventure with "Cowboy Jeff."

 FS-32046 Reading

1. **The main idea of this story is:**
   a. Egypt is a good place for a vacation.
   b. Soams and Spotson solve many crimes.
   c. Pyramids are big.

2. **Soams and Spotson:**
   a. were sore from riding the camel
   b. liked airplanes
   c. enjoyed the pyramids

3. **Soams caught:**
   a. a mummy
   b. Professor Smarty
   c. a baseball

4. **Shillings and piasters are:**
   a. money
   b. types of camels
   c. names of kings

5. **Soams and Spotson probably:**
   a. are good friends
   b. get seasick
   c. don't like each other

* On the back of this paper, draw a different adventure for Soams and Spotson.

1. The main idea of this story is:
   a. Bologna tastes good.
   b. Eating the same food every day is boring.
   c. Books are found in bookstores.

2. Frank wanted his mother to:
   a. make different kinds of sandwiches
   b. clean his room for him
   c. grind her own peanut butter

3. One of Frank's friends said:
   a. He had peanut butter and jelly, too.
   b. He'd trade sandwiches with Frank.
   c. He likes to do math.

4. A bookworm is:
   a. a kind of caterpillar
   b. a book shaped like a worm
   c. a person who reads all the time

5. Frank's mother will probably:
   a. always make the same sandwiches
   b. collect butterflies
   c. make new kinds of sandwiches

* On the back of this paper, write a different ending to this story.

FS-32046 Reading

1. **The main idea of this story is:**
   - a. Baseball is fun.
   - b. Girls can play ball, too.
   - c. Home runs are exciting.

2. **The boys thought Pat was:**
   - a. a good player
   - b. too short
   - c. funny

3. **The Lions played against:**
   - a. the Turtles
   - b. the Tigers
   - c. the Tulips

4. **We'll see how you measure up means:**
   - a. to see how tall you are
   - b. to see how much you weigh
   - c. to see how well you do something

5. **After the game, the boys probably:**
   - a. made Patti feel more welcome
   - b. kicked Patti off the team
   - c. made Patti clean up the whole field

* On the back of this paper, write a paragraph. Tell why you think girls should or shouldn't play sports with boys.

                                  FS-32046 Reading

I think I'll visit Farmer Frank's chicken house tonight. Drumsticks for dinner sounds gooooooood!

Here I come! Ready or not!

That mean fox got two more chickens last night! Poor Clara and Linda! What can I do?

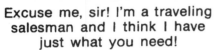

Excuse me, sir! I'm a traveling salesman and I think I have just what you need!

You don't say! I'll be glad to take a look, mister!

Hey! What's this?

Help!

Beep! Come back, you chicken fox!

Haw! That robot chicken I bought is a real winner!

1. **The main idea of this story is:**
    a. Chickens taste good.
    b. It's fun to be a farmer.
    c. You can outfox a fox.

2. **The robot chicken:**
    a. told the fox not to run away
    b. ate the fox
    c. chased the salesman

3. **Who helped the farmer?**
    a. a doctor
    b. a fox
    c. a salesman

4. **A** <u>drumstick</u> **in this story is:**
    a. a stick you can hit a drum with
    b. the leg of a chicken
    c. a game

5. **The fox probably:**
    a. wouldn't return to the farm
    b. wouldn't take a bath
    c. doesn't like chickens

* On the back of this paper, write about another way the farmer could fool Foxy.

1. **The main idea of this story is:**
   - a. Tickets are expensive.
   - b. It's hard to get up early.
   - c. Debbie made a big mistake.

2. **Debbie likes:**
   - a. rock music
   - b. collecting rocks
   - c. buying tickets

3. **The rock show was for:**
   - a. rock collectors
   - b. rock music
   - c. rocking chairs

4. **An <u>auditorium</u> is:**
   - a. a place to keep fish
   - b. a place to see dinosaurs
   - c. a place where people gather for meetings or shows

5. **You can guess that:**
   - a. Debbie was happy to be at the rock show.
   - b. Debbie was very disappointed.
   - c. Debbie wore a red dress that day.

FS-32046 Reading

1. The main idea of this story is:
   a. Everyone wants purple socks.
   b. Ice cream melts fast.
   c. You can get too much of a
      good thing.

2. Diane told people:
   a. about her vacation trip
   b. what to bring to the party
   c. not to sit down

3. At the party they cut the:
   a. cake
   b. ice
   c. turkey

4. Another word for <u>presents</u> is:
   a. fish
   b. dogs
   c. gifts

5. Diane was surprised that:
   a. People came to the party.
   b. It was her birthday.
   c. She got so many purple socks.

* On the back of this paper, write ten things you'd like for your next birthday.

1. The main idea of this story is:
   a. good cheese
   b. running fast
   c. a smart mouse

2. How did the mouse like the cheese?
   a. He liked it a lot.
   b. He threw it out.
   c. He said it had too many holes.

3. What kind of cheese was in the trap?
   a. Swiss cheese
   b. French cheese
   c. American cheese

4. What is a trap?
   a. a dog's bed
   b. something to catch and hold animals
   c. something you use to clean the house

5. You can tell from this story that:
   a. Mice are green.
   b. All cheese has holes.
   c. It can be hard to get rid of a mouse.

* On the back of this paper, write and draw a different ending to this story.

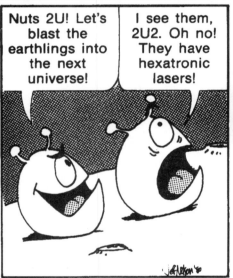

1. The main idea of this story is:
   a. seeing stars
   b. adventures in space
   c. fixing robots

2. The Omega Ogres:
   a. ran back to their planet fast
   b. went home with Reggie and Duke
   c. went on a picnic

3. The Earth ship had:
   a. lasers
   b. razors
   c. phasers

4. An __alien__ is:
   a. a spaceship
   b. a place to keep books
   c. a strange, unfamiliar being

5. Duke and Reggie seem to enjoy:
   a. cheese
   b. adventures
   c. ping pong

* On the back of this paper, draw an adventure for yourself and Reggie.

104

Answer Key

Mrs. Langley watched curiously as her daughter Anne finished dressing one morning. She pulled on her green pants and then turned the pockets inside out. Searching around in her drawer, Anne found an old blue sweater, turned the sleeves out and put it on backwards. Last, she took a rabbit's foot out of a little red box and slipped it around her neck.

"Where are you going dressed like that, Anne?"

"I'm off to school. We're having a math test today and then I have to recite a poem that I haven't even read yet. Mona told me that if I dressed this way, I would have good luck all day. And I'm going to need every bit I can get!"

1. **The main idea of this story is:**
   a. studying for a math test
   b. a girl who believes in good luck charms
   c. dressing up for school

2. **You might think Anne's behavior is somewhat**
   a. unusual.
   b. ordinary.
   c. proper.

3. **What kind of person is Anne?**
   a. a girl who studies hard
   b. a girl who believes in luck
   c. a girl who dresses well

4. **What phrase in the story means "to say from memory"?**
   a. to take a math test
   b. to recite something
   c. read from a book

5. **The story doesn't say, but Anne**
   a. probably had not studied her arithmetic.
   b. didn't know where her new sweater was.
   c. wanted to fool her mother.

(speech bubble) THAT'S THE SILLIEST THING I'VE EVER SEEN!

Page 1

Jeffrey likes to write letters in a secret way so that only his friends know what the message says. Summer vacation was coming to an end, and Jeff thought he had better call a meeting of the Purple Pack Rats Club. They needed to decide where they would go on their last hiking trip. Jeff closed the door to his room and wrote out the plan for each one of the boys. Can you work out the message?

1-A 2-B 3-C 4-D 5-E 6-F 7-G 8-H 9-I 10-J 11-K 12-L 13-M
14-N 15-O 16-P 17-Q 18-R 19-S 20-T 21-U 22-V 23-W 24-X
25-Y 26-Z

M E E T I N G   T H U R S D A Y
13 5 5 20 9 14 7   20 8 21 18 19 4 1 25
N I G H T :   S E V E N
14 9 7 8 20   19 5 22 5 14

1. **The main idea of this story is:**
   a. writing secret messages to friends
   b. taking a vacation in September
   c. learning how to read and write

2. **Hiking can be a sport or a**
   a. race.
   b. hobby.
   c. dance.

3. **What month do you think it is?**
   a. November
   b. June
   c. August

4. **In the story "close" means "to shut". "Close" also means**
   a. far away.
   b. near to.
   c. things you wear.

5. **The story doesn't tell, but you might think Jeff**
   a. was President of the Purple Pack Rats.
   b. didn't want girls in the club.
   c. was younger than the other boys.

(speech bubble) BE SURE TO EAT THE MESSAGE AFTER READING IT.

Page 2

"What is this mess in my living room?" Mrs. Rogers shrieked. "Look at the walls, the rug, and Mr. Roger's favorite chair! Someone has a lot of explaining to do."

"Ernie invited us to his magic show," Betsey told Mrs. Rogers. "First he tried the tablecloth trick. He put some eggs, juice and sandwiches on the tablecloth and then with a wave of his hand, pulled it off. The trick didn't work. Everything was supposed to land on the table, but instead the food flew in every direction. We tried to clean it up, but the rug drank the milk. The windows were so hot today, the eggs just about fried the minute they hit the glass. One trick did work, though. Ernie made the canary disappear and now we can't find it."

1. **The main idea of this story is:**
   a. a canary disappears
   b. Ernie gives an un-magic show
   c. frying eggs on the window

2. **"Mother shrieked at the sight." You might guess that**
   a. Mother was in the kitchen during the show.
   b. she was away from the house during the show.
   c. she was talking to Betsey during the show.

3. **What happened to the milk?**
   a. it soaked into the carpet
   b. it spilled on the chair
   c. it stayed in the glass

4. **Spell "flew" a different way and you will have**
   a. a word that means upset.
   b. a word that means ill.
   c. a word that means go away.

5. **How do you think mother feels about Ernie?**
   a. glad he has so much imagination
   b. angry because the canary has egg on it
   c. angry because the house is disorderly

(speech bubble) WHERE COULD THAT BIRD HAVE GONE?

Page 3

"They're having a 'Most Beautiful Cat' contest in the park on Sunday and I'm going to enter Oliver," Sally told her big brother.

"That animal of yours is the poorest excuse for a cat that I have ever seen in my life! Oliver can't even purr very well," Phil laughed.

"Just you wait, Phil. When I get finished, Ollie will win a prize." Sally picked up the cat and went into her room. She mixed a few colors of her fingerpaints and then rubbed them into Oliver's fur, adding a few extra dots here and there. "What do you think now, Phil?"

Phil laughed so hard tears rolled down his face. "That's great, Sally. Only now you can't enter Oliver as a cat. He looks just like a ladybug with a tail."

1. **The main idea of the story is:**
   a. entering a cat in a contest
   b. a fingerpainting project
   c. a cat that doesn't purr

2. **Phil was sure that Oliver would not**
   a. win the contest.
   b. learn to purr.
   c. lose his fur.

3. **What doesn't the story tell?**
   a. how Phil felt about the cat
   b. what Sally put on Oliver's fur
   c. what kind of cat Oliver was

4. **"Poorest excuse for a cat" means**
   a. Oliver is not a very beautiful cat.
   b. Oliver looks just like a lady bug.
   c. Phil doesn't like cats.

5. **What colors do you think Sally painted Oliver?**
   a. black with green dots
   b. red with purple dots
   c. red with black dots

Page 4

Answer Key

Name ·

"Jonathan, will you please go to the store and get me some green beans, juice and ham? Hurry, I have to fix dinner soon."

On his way into town, Jonathan passed Mervin's Hobby Shop where a big green and yellow box in the window caught his eye. "That must be the new model Zip-A-Long Bi-Plane. I better go in just in case Mervin needs me to help him put it together."

Two hours passed before Jonathan realized he was supposed to be home by five. "Hm-m-m, where was I going before I got side-tracked? I'll go home and ask Mom. She'll know."

"You did it again, Jonathan? Every time you get near that hobby shop, your memory shuts off like a light switch. What will I do with you?"

1. **The main idea of this story is:**
   a. making a trip to the store
   ⓑ a boy who gets side-tracked
   c. building a bi-plane

2. **Jonathan was not very good at**
   a. deciding what to buy.
   b. finding the store.
   ⓒ remembering where he was going.

3. **When Jonathan went by the hobby shop he**
   a. bought some beans and ham.
   ⓑ helped Mervin build a bi-plane.
   c. called his mother at home.

4. **A "way" can be a route to get to town. "Weigh" means:**
   a. thinned milk
   ⓑ put something on a scale
   c. don't go too fast

5. **You might think Jonathan was**
   a. not very smart.
   b. a bad boy.
   ⓒ sometimes forgetful.

Page 5

Name

"Our homework for tonight is to find out about our last names. How did we get the name 'Shields', Dad?"

"I don't know if this is exactly true, Nora, because the facts have never been written down, but I think this is the way the story goes. A very long time ago, one of my ancestors was a farmer in the hill country in England. His name was Henmonger which means he 'raised ducks and chickens'. He got tired of that work and moved to a village where he then made armor. Most people in those days took a last name that told about the kind of job they did. So, Mr. Henmonger changed his name to Mr. Shields because that is what he made - shields of armor. That's how we got our name."

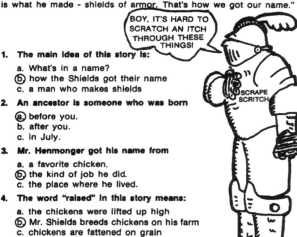

1. **The main idea of this story is:**
   a. What's in a name?
   ⓑ how the Shields got their name
   c. a man who makes shields

2. **An ancestor is someone who was born**
   ⓐ before you.
   b. after you.
   c. in July.

3. **Mr. Henmonger got his name from**
   a. a favorite chicken.
   ⓑ the kind of job he did.
   c. the place where he lived.

4. **The word "raised" in this story means:**
   a. the chickens were lifted up high
   ⓑ Mr. Shields breeds chickens on his farm
   c. chickens are fattened on grain

5. **From the story you might guess that**
   ⓐ Mr. Shields kept his job making armor.
   b. raising chickens is not a good job.
   c. this story is not true.

Page 6

Name

On the day I was born, my uncle, grandfather, father, third cousin and another distant relative were at the hospital staring at me through the nursery window. "I think he looks just like me," Uncle Herman said. "You're mistaken, Herman," Cousin Ralph chimed in. "He's the image of his great-grandfather Melvin. No doubt about it!" Grandfather George got in the last word. "That boy's a Delancey for sure. Just look at that nose."

"I'll settle this," my father said calmly. "All of you wait here while I go down and sign the birth record."

And that is how I got my name: John Melvin Ralph George Herman Delancey Grant. Everyone calls me "J.G." for short.

1. **The main idea of this story is:**
   ⓐ how J.G. got his name
   b. visiting a new born baby
   c. birth records

2. **A relative is someone who is a member**
   a. of a private club.
   b. of your church.
   ⓒ of your family.

3. **Which relative do you think is named John?**
   a. the grandfather
   ⓑ the father
   c. the uncle

4. **"Record" here means certificate. Another "record" is**
   a. a return.
   ⓑ an album.
   c. a direction.

5. **The story doesn't say, but you can guess that:**
   a. J.G. didn't like his long name.
   ⓑ Father tried to please all the relatives.
   c. Grandfather didn't know Ralph very well.

Page 7

Name

Once a week, mostly on Fridays, our teacher gives us different kinds of puzzles to work out. Sometimes we have mind-benders and tongue-twisters, or crosswords and riddles, but my favorites are the jumbles. The teacher asks a question and then we unscramble the letters in the words to find the answer. I'm such a smart girl, I usually know the answer before I even work out the puzzle. One time, though, the teacher tried to fool me. Yesterday, this was the question we had to solve: "What is it that smells the worst?" Can you put the letters in order and find an answer?

HTIS ZULZPE AHS ON NSARWE
<u>THIS</u> <u>PUZZLE</u> <u>HAS</u> <u>NO</u> <u>ANSWER</u>

1. **The main idea of this story is:**
   a. solving crosswords in class
   ⓑ a puzzling jumble
   c. a good question for a puzzle

2. **Jumbles are puzzles where**
   a. words are upside down.
   ⓑ letters are not in the right order.
   c. only eight letter words are used.

3. **When did the class work on puzzles?**
   a. whenever they wanted
   b. mostly on Mondays
   ⓒ on the last school day of the week

4. **A "smell" is a**
   a. color.
   ⓑ scent.
   c. cent.

5. **You might guess that the girl**
   a. didn't know how to unscramble words.
   b. never learned to read.
   ⓒ knew a lot of riddles.

Page 8

FS-32046 Reading

Answer Key

Name _____

Bucky Thornton drives me crazy sometimes. I never seem to be able to get a straight answer out of him. A simple "yes" or "no" to my questions would do most of the time. But Bucky can't resist including a silly saying or two in his answer. The other day I asked Bucky, "Why didn't Tony come to the baseball meeting yesterday?"

"Let me tell you what happened, James. Tony lost his glasses. He's as blind as a bat, you know, and probably couldn't find his way out of a paper bag without those glasses. After he fumbled around like an owl in daylight, Tony finally found his glasses just where he left them - on top of his head."

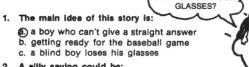

WHERE ARE THOSE GLASSES?

1. **The main idea of this story is:**
   ⓐ a boy who can't give a straight answer
   b. getting ready for the baseball game
   c. a blind boy loses his glasses

2. **A silly saying could be:**
   a. dangerous
   ⓑ humorous
   c. furious

3. **It is impossible for Bucky to give**
   a. an answer that is right.
   ⓑ an answer that is to the point.
   c. an answer that is long.

4. **To "fumble like an owl in daylight" means:**
   a. Owls need glasses during the day.
   ⓑ Owls probably don't see well in daylight.
   c. Owls cannot hunt very well.

5. **From the story, you cannot tell:**
   a. what Bucky said to James
   b. that Bucky uses silly sayings
   ⓒ where the baseball meeting was held

Page 9

Name _____

When I was little, I used to think that if I grew up and became a dentist, I would never have to have my teeth drilled again. Or if I became a doctor, I would never be unhealthy another day in my life. Or maybe I would be a teacher and then I would never have to study anymore.

One day, my dentist pointed to his mouth and said, "See this tooth Doug? It seems the nerve died and now it will have to be drilled." If this could happen to a dentist, I figured a doctor could probably get sick, too. What was there left for me to be when I grew up?

I guess the only thing I would be is a grown-up. And the only thing I would not be is a little boy.

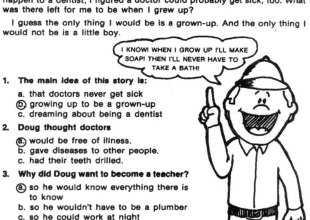

I KNOW! WHEN I GROW UP I'LL MAKE SOAP! THEN I'LL NEVER HAVE TO TAKE A BATH!

1. **The main idea of this story is:**
   a. that doctors never get sick
   ⓑ growing up to be a grown-up
   c. dreaming about being a dentist

2. **Doug thought doctors**
   ⓐ would be free of illness.
   b. gave diseases to other people.
   c. had their teeth drilled.

3. **Why did Doug want to become a teacher?**
   ⓐ so he would know everything there is to know
   b. so he wouldn't have to be a plumber
   c. so he could work at night

4. **Your mouth has 32 teeth. What else has teeth?**
   a. a toothbrush
   ⓑ a comb
   c. a newborn baby

5. **Doug would probably think that policemen**
   ⓐ never went to jail.
   b. never got any sleep.
   c. never gave out tickets.

Page 10

Name _____

Janet felt great on this bright, sunny morning. "I don't even mind going to school. It's so pretty today." She whistled "Yankee Doodle Dandy" and skipped off down the street. At the corner of Wiley Street, Tommy Gray popped out from behind a gate:

" 'A whistling girl and crowing hen
Always come to no good end...' "

My mom told me that little girls who whistle will grow a beard and my mother is always right! You better be careful, Janet!"

"Go away, Tommy. That doesn't really happen. It's just a silly superstition that someone made up a long time ago to scare girls."

1. **The main idea of this story is:**
   ⓐ a boy who believes in superstitions
   b. Janet dancing on her way to school
   c. whistling girls grow beards

2. **Years ago, some superstitions developed**
   a. from months of hard work.
   ⓑ to frighten people.
   c. from songs and dances.

3. **Tommy thought his mother**
   a. would like to meet Janet.
   b. didn't know much about girls.
   ⓒ always told the truth.

4. **Which would be an example of a superstition?**
   a. a fear of going to school
   b. a lady in a full moon
   ⓒ fear of Friday the 13th

5. **The story doesn't say, but Janet most likely**
   a. learned to sing instead of whistle.
   ⓑ went right on whistling down the street.
   c. grew a beard the next day.

Page 11

Name _____

"Have a piece of cake, Mom, and a cookie too. I made them myself," said Lucy, passing the plate across the table. "I learned how to bake these in my science class. Our teacher has been demonstrating how we can better use natural foods in everything we eat."

"Ah-h-h! Lucy, what is this in my cookie? It doesn't look like a chocolate chip."

"It's an earthworm, Mother. Earthworms and insects are the foods of the future. Just think, you may never have to go to the grocery store again!"

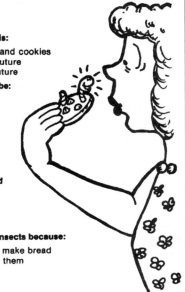

1. **The main idea of this story is:**
   a. making earthworm cakes and cookies
   b. planning classes for the future
   ⓒ some new foods in our future

2. **Another natural food might be:**
   a. a candy bar
   ⓑ a beetle
   c. a root beer

3. **Mother probably didn't like**
   a. chocolate chip cookies.
   b. Lucy's English teacher.
   ⓒ the taste of the cookies.

4. **The opposite of a natural food would be a**
   a. canned food.
   ⓑ man-made food.
   c. sun-grown food.

5. **Many years ago, people ate insects because:**
   a. they did not know how to make bread
   b. they needed to get rid of them
   ⓒ they were a healthy food

Page 12

107

Answer Key

Name _____

"You have a lot of ability, Arthur. I hope you will always take good care of it. Use it wisely and it will grow along with you."

Arthur wasn't really sure what the teacher meant, but he decided to take her advice and be extra careful with his ability. So he took it home and put it in the closet. "It'll be safe in here for a long time."

The years passed. One day, Arthur had to take an important test for a summer job. "I'll go home and get my ability and be right back," he told the man. But his ability wasn't in the closet anymore. "Oh, no! I've never used my ability all this time and now it's gone. I should have known I needed to use it every day so it would develop with me!"

1. **The main idea of this story is:**
   a. hiding ability in the closet
   ⓑ the ability that never grew
   c. Arthur loses a summer job

2. **A person's ability is usually a special**
   ⓐ skill.
   b. operation.
   c. teacher.

3. **Why did Arthur put his ability in the closet?**
   a. because that is where it belongs
   b. because his teacher told him
   ⓒ for safekeeping

4. **A "wise" person would be someone who**
   a. belongs in jail.
   ⓑ tries hard.
   c. is simple.

5. **From the story, you can tell that Arthur did not**
   a. know how to take a test.
   ⓑ understand what the teacher was saying.
   c. want to develop his ability.

Page 13

Name _____

"I sure am getting tired of everyone walking in here every morning and gritting their teeth right in my face," the mirror reflected.

"Me, too," gurgled the faucet. "Look at this mess in my sink. It doesn't drain like it used to when it was young. All that toothpaste and shaving cream has clogged the pipes."

"I have the answer, Sir Faucet. Tomorrow morning, put a lock on your 'Cold'. If only hot water rushes out, steam will billow up and cover me with fog. No one brushes their teeth with hot water. This will be a triumph for mirrors and faucets everywhere!"

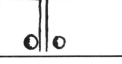

1. **The main idea of this story is:**
   ⓐ a mirror and faucet plot a plan
   b. turning on the hot water
   c. shaving in a mirror

2. **The sink had probably been in the bathroom**
   a. just a few weeks.
   ⓑ several years.
   c. since day before yesterday.

3. **What caused the pipes to clog?**
   ⓐ thick toothpaste
   b. dirty water
   c. a bar of soap

4. **To "grit" your teeth means to**
   a. brush them up and down.
   ⓑ grind them around.
   c. click them together.

5. **On line 4, who does the word "it" refer to?**
   ⓐ the sink
   b. the faucet
   c. the pipes

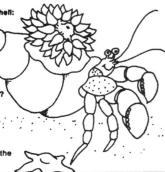

Page 14

Name _____

"You could be a very good writer someday, Lisa," Mrs. Roberts told her. "But you need to learn to use more adjectives to describe your characters. Today, write me a story about what you would like to do this summer." A little later Lisa returned her paragraph to the teacher, and this is what she wrote:

> I want to go to camp again this summer. Last summer I rode a horse named "Happy New Year". He was the color of a cloudy sky with splashes of milk and he could run like lightning. I learned how to handle him so well, that after a few weeks I didn't need a saddle anymore. Someday I would like to work at that camp.

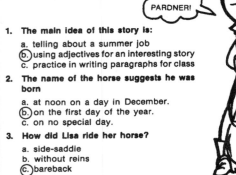

1. **The main idea of this story is:**
   a. telling about a summer job
   ⓑ using adjectives for an interesting story
   c. practice in writing paragraphs for class

2. **The name of the horse suggests he was born**
   a. at noon on a day in December.
   ⓑ on the first day of the year.
   c. on no special day.

3. **How did Lisa ride her horse?**
   a. side-saddle
   b. without reins
   ⓒ bareback

4. **To "run like lightning" means to**
   a. run during a rainstorm.
   ⓑ run very fast.
   c. run over rooftops.

5. **From the clues you can tell the horse's color was**
   ⓐ gray with white spots.
   b. cloudy and gray.
   c. gray with milk splashed on.

Page 15

Name _____

Hermit Crabs

Lobsters, crabs, shrimps and barnacles are crustaceans. A crustacean is an animal with a crust. Most crustaceans have at least ten legs and four feelers. They live in water and breathe with gills as fish do.

Although a hermit crab is a crab, it looks more like a small lobster. The hind part of a hermit crab is not protected by a strong crusty shell, so it must use the shell of a sea snail to cover its soft parts. The kind of shell it uses depends on where it lives and upon its size. As the crab grows each shelter becomes too tight and it must search for a larger one. The hermit anchors itself inside its new home by means of its rear pair of tiny hooklike legs. The large pair of front legs has claws with which the hermit catches food—tiny fish and dead animal matter. These front claws also form a closed front door when it has gone completely inside the shell. Hermit crabs often have partners who live on their shell and act as camouflage. A sea anemone often looks like a beautiful flower growing on a shell. It enjoys eating scraps from the hermit crab's meals.

1. **This story is mainly about:**
   a. ocean creatures
   b. mammals in the sea
   ⓒ shell-dwelling crabs

2. **When the hermit crab is without a shell:**
   ⓐ it is unprotected
   b. it enjoys swimming
   c. it is safe from danger

3. **Hind legs of the hermit crab:**
   a. catch food
   ⓑ hold it in the shell
   c. are used for protection

4. **What word means "to hold in place"?**
   a. cover
   ⓑ anchor
   c. camouflage

5. **You can tell that hermit crabs:**
   a. have large, powerful hind legs
   b. must come to the surface to breathe
   ⓒ have many homes in a lifetime

Page 16

Answer Key

Name _____

Polar Bears

Polar bears are smaller than you are at birth. They weigh one pound and are ten inches long. When full grown, polar bears can weigh seven hundred pounds. Newborn bears are helpless. In winter the female bear goes into a cave in an iceberg where she gives birth to one or two cubs. In springtime they leave the ice cave. Their white fur blends in with the Arctic ice and snow. Oil in their fur keeps them warm and dry. Fur on the bottom of their feet stops them from slipping on the ice. The polar bear has a different shape than most other bears. His head is smaller, his neck longer and his body more slender. This body shape helps make the Polar bear an excellent swimmer. They have been sighted in the ocean hundreds of miles from shore.

Polar bears eat plants, berries, seals, walruses and fish. Cubs learn to hunt and swim. They must learn everything they need to know in two years. The mother bear chases the cubs away when they reach two years of age. They must learn to survive on their own.

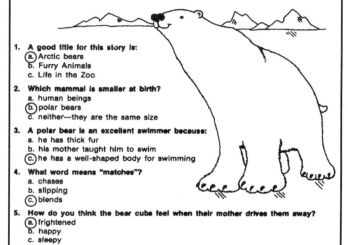

1. **A good title for this story is:**
   a. Arctic bears *(circled)*
   b. Furry Animals
   c. Life in the Zoo

2. **Which mammal is smaller at birth?**
   a. human beings
   b. polar bears *(circled)*
   c. neither—they are the same size

3. **A polar bear is an excellent swimmer because:**
   a. he has thick fur
   b. his mother taught him to swim
   c. he has a well-shaped body for swimming *(circled)*

4. **What word means "matches"?**
   a. chases
   b. slipping
   c. blends *(circled)*

5. **How do you think the bear cubs feel when their mother drives them away?**
   a. frightened *(circled)*
   b. happy
   c. sleepy

Page 17

Name _____

Turtles

Each kind of turtle has a different looking shell, but all turtles have shells. Turtles are born with a soft covering of shell and bone. As the turtle grows its shell hardens and grows too. The shell offers protection from enemies.

A map turtle has a wide, flat shell with bumpy edges. A soft-shelled turtle's shell looks like a green pancake. A box turtle has a high, round shell that can close up like a box. But if the box turtle eats too much it gets too big for its shell and its fat legs keep popping out. However, most turtles can grow to weigh over two hundred pounds.

Sea turtles spend all of their lives in water with one exception. They must come up on beaches to lay their eggs in a dry place high above the water. The female may lay as many as one hundred eggs that look much like a pile of ping pong balls before she covers them with sand.

1. **This story is mainly about:**
   a. how turtles are different *(circled)*
   b. how turtles protect themselves
   c. where turtles lay eggs

2. **If a box turtle eats too much:**
   a. he outgrows his shell *(circled)*
   b. he grows a larger shell
   c. his shell becomes soft

3. **Where does the sea turtle lay eggs?**
   a. shallow water
   b. tidepools
   c. dry beach *(circled)*

4. **Which word in the story means "gives"?**
   a. covering
   b. offers *(circled)*
   c. popping

5. **From reading the story you can tell that:**
   a. turtles cannot protect themselves
   b. turtles can weigh up to fifty pounds
   c. turtles can be identified by their shells *(circled)*

Page 18

Name _____

Orangutans

The orangutan sleeps high in a tree. His bed is made of leafy branches. He holds on tightly with his fingers and toes while sleeping. The five foot tall, one hundred pound animal has red, stringy hair. Orangutans are primates just like you. Monkeys, apes and man are in the primate group of animals. Orangutans spend most of their time in trees swinging from branch to branch. Their long arms help them swing through the trees searching for bird's eggs, bark, leaves and fruit to eat.

Orangutans are frequently seen in zoos. They live rather well in captivity, if they have the right food and proper care. The orangutan is considered to be an endangered animal. Too many have been caught and sold. Now they are protected by law and may not be captured anymore.

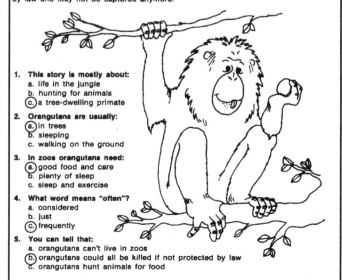

1. **This story is mostly about:**
   a. life in the jungle
   b. hunting for animals
   c. a tree-dwelling primate *(circled)*

2. **Orangutans are usually:**
   a. in trees *(circled)*
   b. sleeping
   c. walking on the ground

3. **In zoos orangutans need:**
   a. good food and care *(circled)*
   b. plenty of sleep
   c. sleep and exercise

4. **What word means "often"?**
   a. considered
   b. just
   c. frequently *(circled)*

5. **You can tell that:**
   a. orangutans can't live in zoos
   b. orangutans could all be killed if not protected by law *(circled)*
   c. orangutans hunt animals for food

Page 19

Name _____

Dogs

The dog has been man's best friend for thousands of years. They are usually friendly and learn to mind well. All over the world, dogs are trained to help people in work and play. They are ranked fifth in intelligence and were the first animal to be tamed by man. They make good guards and can protect people and their possessions. Sometimes dogs are used to help policemen in their work. Specially trained dogs lead blind persons. Dogs like to be with people and are especially happy when they are with children.

A puppy should be house-trained as soon as it is taken from its mother. He must learn to follow directions. First he should be taught how to walk when wearing a leash. Then the puppy should be taught to come when his master calls. Dogs can be taught to follow many commands. A dog should be rewarded with kind words and pats when he does something right.

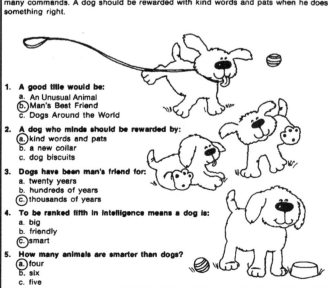

1. **A good title would be:**
   a. An Unusual Animal
   b. Man's Best Friend *(circled)*
   c. Dogs Around the World

2. **A dog who minds should be rewarded by:**
   a. kind words and pats *(circled)*
   b. a new collar
   c. dog biscuits

3. **Dogs have been man's friend for:**
   a. twenty years
   b. hundreds of years
   c. thousands of years *(circled)*

4. **To be ranked fifth in intelligence means a dog is:**
   a. big
   b. friendly
   c. smart *(circled)*

5. **How many animals are smarter than dogs?**
   a. four *(circled)*
   b. six
   c. five

Page 20

109

FS-32046 Reading

Answer Key

Name _____

Bats

Bats are the only flying mammals. The small mouse-like animals have long, thin fingers. Thin skin that spreads between the fingers forms the wings. There are over two thousand kinds of bats. Some people are afraid of bats. They think bats will fly into them. This is not true because bats can "see" in total darkness. They can't see with their eyes so they make sounds as they fly. These sounds are too high for us to hear. The sounds echo and the bat can tell when it is coming close to something. Hundreds of bats can fly in a dark cave without ever crashing into the walls or into one another.

Hind claws help the bat hang upside down for sleeping. Most bats are nocturnal animals so they sleep during the day and hunt for food at night. They fly through the darkness scooping up insects by the hundreds. Bats help man by eating insect pests.

1. This story is mostly about:
   a. nocturnal animals
   b. a flying mammal
   c. hunting for bats

2. Most bats sleep during the:
   a. day
   b. night
   c. winter

3. How many kinds of bats are there?
   a. two thousand or more
   b. no one knows
   c. one hundred

4. What word in the story means "correct"?
   a. another
   b. true
   c. helpful

5. You can tell that:
   a. people should be afraid of bats
   b. people should not be afraid of bats
   c. bats and birds have the same kind of wings

Page 21

Name _____

Dolphins

The dolphin is one of the fastest swimmers in the sea. Their powerful tails beat up and down when they swim. The tail and flippers are used for steering. Their mouths are curved to look like a big, happy grin. These friendly mammals are related to whales and porpoises. Dolphins can stay under water for four to six minutes. While sleeping they come to the surface to breathe without waking up. Breathing is done through a blowhole on top of the dolphin's head. The Bottlenose dolphins are seven to eleven feet long and weigh three to seven hundred pounds.

Baby dolphins are born tail first under the water. Other dolphins gather around to help. They help the baby go up to the surface for air and guard it against sharks. A young dolphin stays with its mother until it is about eighteen months old.

A dolphin's language is made up of clicks, whistles and grunts. These sounds echo back to tell them where to find food. They see with their ears, as bats do. Man has not yet learned to understand dolphin language. Dolphins like to be with humans and have been trained to help people.

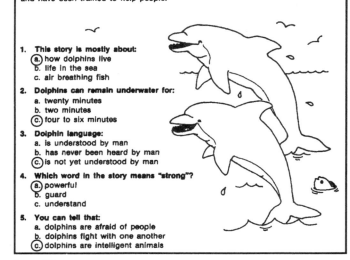

1. This story is mostly about:
   a. how dolphins live
   b. life in the sea
   c. air breathing fish

2. Dolphins can remain underwater for:
   a. twenty minutes
   b. two minutes
   c. four to six minutes

3. Dolphin language:
   a. is understood by man
   b. has never been heard by man
   c. is not yet understood by man

4. Which word in the story means "strong"?
   a. powerful
   b. guard
   c. understand

5. You can tell that:
   a. dolphins are afraid of people
   b. dolphins fight with one another
   c. dolphins are intelligent animals

Page 22

Name _____

Cats

Fierce lions and tigers are like your pet cat in many ways. All cats belong to the same cat family. Helpless newborns are blind and must be cared for by the mother cat. Cats have a rough tongue that cleans their fur. The mother washes the kittens until they are big enough to keep themselves clean. She watches over them until they are old enough to hunt for food. All cats are meat-eaters. They have an instinct for hunting.

Cats have round heads and small noses. Their strong legs help them to run and jump. All cats have five toes on their front paws and four on the hind paws. Each toe has a sharp, curved claw. Padded feet allow the cat to move quietly. The cheetah is a member of the cat family. In a burst of speed it can run seventy miles per hour! The cheetah is the world's fastest running animal.

Cats' eyes change according to the light. When it is dark their pupils open wide to let them see in the dark. Cats can see quite well in the dark. Most cats hunt for food at night.

1. This story is mostly about:
   a. the cat family
   b. how cats hunt for food
   c. newborn cats

2. Strong legs, padded feet and claws:
   a. are not important to cats
   b. are only found on lions and tigers
   c. help all cats hunt for meat

3. On their front paws cats have:
   a. four toes
   b. five toes
   c. three toes

4. Which word in the story means "not smooth"?
   a. fierce
   b. padded
   c. rough

5. Your pet cat is:
   a. exactly like a cheetah
   b. in the same family as lions and tigers
   c. not a meat-eater

Page 23

Name _____

Skunks

Skunks are known for their strong, unpleasant odor. The skunk uses his scent to protect itself from enemies. An animal sprayed by a skunk will smell awful for days. Before spraying, the skunk warns that he is frightened by stamping his feet, clicking his teeth and hissing. It raises its tail to spray. The spray can reach thirteen feet, and the skunk usually hits whatever he wants to spray. The spray is not harmful, but it smells awful, makes your eyes burn and cannot be washed off.

Skunks live in burrows or hollow logs. They are nocturnal animals who roam around at night to find food. Skunks will eat almost anything. They turn over rocks and sniff around to find insects, nuts, fruit and reptiles. In the cold winter, skunks eat very little and sleep for several days at a time. They find a mate, and baby skunks are born in the spring.

The striped skunk is about the size of a large cat. It has a pointed nose and an arched back. Its thick, shiny black fur has two white stripes down the back. The skunk has short legs and walks as though its shoes are too tight. Skunks are easy to identify because of their coloring. If you see a skunk, do not get too close—you might get sprayed!

1. The best name for this story is:
   a. How to Catch a Skunk
   b. Where Skunks Live
   c. All About Skunks

2. Skunks live in the:
   a. woods
   b. desert
   c. tops of trees

3. The skunk:
   a. sprays without any warning
   b. stamps, clicks his teeth and hisses
   c. runs away when frightened

4. What word in the story means "lifts"?
   a. warns
   b. raises
   c. sprays

5. You can tell that the skunk:
   a. makes a good pet
   b. looks like a cat
   c. can protect itself

Page 24

Answer Key

Dinosaurs

Tyrannosaurus Rex (tie-ron-oh-sawr-us rex) was the most fierce animal that ever walked on the earth. It was eighteen to twenty feet tall and walked on its powerful hind legs. Its jaws were four feet long and contained long, sharp teeth. Its teeth and strong jaws were used for biting and tearing apart meat. This gigantic, meat-eating dinosaur killed animals, ate them and then slept for several days. Other dinosaurs were afraid of it.

We know dinosaurs lived long ago but no man has ever seen one. Dinosaurs lived millions of years before people appeared on earth. Fossils have told us the story of the dinosaurs. Fossils are the hardened remains of animals that lived many years ago. Scientists study fossils for information about the past. They found out how dinosaurs looked and what the land was like in dinosaur times. Bones of the Tyrannosaurous Rex were found in the state of Montana. Millions of years ago, when dinosaurs lived there, it was a warm, swampy jungle. Much of what is now the United States was covered by ocean water.

Scientists have not figured out why dinosaurs disappeared. Perhaps the jungles got colder and the dinosaurs could not live in cold weather. Some scientists believe small, furry animals ate dinosaur eggs so baby dinosaurs did not hatch and grow. Perhaps there was not enough food for the giant animals. Dinosaur skeletons can be seen in many museums.

1. **This story is mostly about:**
   a. dinosaur eggs
   b. **animals who lived before man**
   c. cave man and the dinosaurs

2. **Millions of years ago the land was:**
   a. colder
   b. **warmer**
   c. about the same as now

3. **We know about dinosaurs from:**
   a. museums
   b. old photographs
   c. **fossils**

4. **The word "disappeared" in the story means:**
   a. passed from sight
   b. figured
   c. **no longer alive**

5. **You can tell that dinosaurs:**
   a. **hatched from eggs**
   b. were playful
   c. can live in any climate

Page 25

Toads

Toads spend the cold winter buried underground. They come out of hibernation in the warm springtime. Toads and frogs look much alike. Frogs have smooth skin and toads have rough, bumpy skin. Some people think you can get warts from touching toads, but that is not true.

Toads eat live insects. They will only eat things that move. Many kinds of toads have long, sticky tongues. The toad suddenly shoots out his tongue and the insect is caught. It cannot get away because it is stuck to the toad's tongue.

Toads gulp in air and force it into a sac in their throats. The toad makes a singing sound as it lets the air out. This song is a signal that it is breeding time. Toad eggs are lain in shallow water. Many are eaten by other animals. The rest hatch into tadpoles. Three months later the tadpole has changed into an air-breathing toad. Animals who are born to breathe underwater and later grow into air-breathing animals are called amphibians.

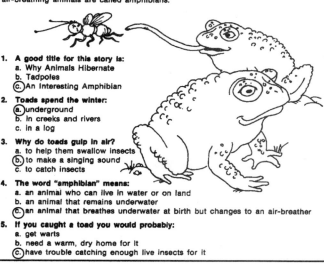

1. **A good title for this story is:**
   a. Why Animals Hibernate
   b. Tadpoles
   c. **An Interesting Amphibian**

2. **Toads spend the winter:**
   a. **underground**
   b. in creeks and rivers
   c. in a log

3. **Why do toads gulp in air?**
   a. to help them swallow insects
   b. **to make a singing sound**
   c. to catch insects

4. **The word "amphibian" means:**
   a. an animal who can live in water or on land
   b. an animal that remains underwater
   c. **an animal that breathes underwater at birth but changes to an air-breather**

5. **If you caught a toad you would probably:**
   a. get warts
   b. need a warm, dry home for it
   c. **have trouble catching enough live insects for it**

Page 26

Fireflies

A firefly is an unusual insect. It has a yellow light that flashes on and off on the back part of its body. The firefly is about an inch long. It can be found in warm, grassy places in the summer. At night you can see their small lights blinking on and off. The male firefly blinks his light first. When he does this he is signaling to a female firefly that he is looking for a mate. If a female is nearby she will signal back by flashing her light. The lights are used to help the male and female fireflies get together.

Scientists know the light is used to bring the male and female firefly together. They do not understand exactly how the tiny insect makes its own light. The light is similar to a flashlight. There is a reflector behind the light and a clear place in front of it. The light goes on and is reflected out through the clear area on its body. People enjoy watching fireflies on warm summer nights.

1. **A good name for this story is:**
   a. Insect Pests
   b. How to Catch Fireflies
   c. **Insects with Flashing Lights**

2. **When do fireflies mate?**
   a. **on warm summer nights**
   b. during hibernation
   c. during the day

3. **Scientists don't know:**
   a. how a flashlight works
   b. **how fireflies make their light**
   c. what fireflies use their light for

4. **The word "together" means the opposite of:**
   a. nearby
   b. **apart**
   c. friendly

5. **Fireflies use their lights to:**
   a. frighten other insects
   b. **communicate**
   c. make them fly faster

Page 27

Porcupines

Can porcupines throw their quills? No, they cannot, but the quills do come out easily. The body of the porcupine is covered by quills that are several inches long. Each quill has a barb on the end like a fishhook. When a quill gets stuck in another animal it is very painful.

Rats, squirrels and porcupines are in the rodent family. They have big front teeth and will gnaw on almost anything. They love to gnaw on things that are salty. When people touch things they leave a tiny bit of salty perspiration. The porcupine gnaws on old shoes, tools or whatever he can find that people have touched. They eat fruit, vegetables, flowers and twigs, but never other animals. At times porcupines are troublesome pests. They gnaw on the bark of trees in the woods where they live. This causes many trees to die.

American porcupines are slow and clumsy on the ground. They are fast swimmers and good climbers.

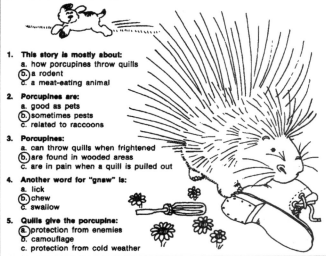

1. **This story is mostly about:**
   a. how porcupines throw quills
   b. **a rodent**
   c. a meat-eating animal

2. **Porcupines are:**
   a. good as pets
   b. **sometimes pests**
   c. related to raccoons

3. **Porcupines:**
   a. can throw quills when frightened
   b. **are found in wooded areas**
   c. are in pain when a quill is pulled out

4. **Another word for "gnaw" is:**
   a. lick
   b. **chew**
   c. swallow

5. **Quills give the porcupine:**
   a. **protection from enemies**
   b. camouflage
   c. protection from cold weather

Page 28

Answer Key

Name

Raccoons

Raccoons are easy to identify. They have five to seven rings of black fur around their bushy tails. Black fur is also around the raccoon's eyes in the shape of a mask. These nocturnal animals hunt in the dark for food.

Raccoons hiss, snarl and growl when they are angry. When they grunt and make a shrill sound they are happy. They can be fierce fighters. Long claws, forty teeth and strong jaws help the raccoon defend itself. Raccoons have five long fingers on their front paws. They can open latches, turn doorknobs and twist bottle caps. They are intelligent, curious animals who like to poke into things.

Birds, tadpoles, fish, fruit and vegetables are eaten by raccoons. They slosh their food around in water before eating it. Scientists do not think that raccoons are washing their food to clean it. They believe that raccoons wet their food for another reason, but they do not know exactly why. Some scientists believe raccoons can swallow wet food easier. Others think that raccoons learned to slosh food in water because they often find food in water. Maybe they do it just for fun!

1. The best title for this story is:
   a. The Raccoon—A Curious Animal
   b. Animals who Live in Trees
   c. Caring for a Pet Raccoon

2. Raccoons can:
   a. not swim
   b. open all sorts of things
   c. not see at night

3. Scientists:
   a. know raccoons will only eat clean food
   b. have never studied raccoons
   c. are not sure why raccoons wet their food

4. "Intelligent" means:
   a. careful
   b. curious
   c. smart

5. Raccoons are:
   a. intelligent and curious
   b. safe in their homes at night
   c. afraid of eating dirty food

Page 29

Name

Rattlesnakes

Rattlesnakes are found in almost every state in the United States. The largest, most dangerous rattlesnake is the diamondback. It grows to be five to six feet long. Snakes are cold-blooded. They are warm when they are in a warm place and cold when they are in a cold place. Snakes often sun themselves on a warm rock to warm their bodies after a cool night. In winter snakes hibernate so they do not freeze to death.

All rattlesnakes have heads shaped like a triangle. They shed their skins as they grow bigger, and they continue to shed when full grown. They rub their heads on something rough to make a hole in the old skin. The skin peels back as they slowly wiggle out of the old skin. You may find a snakeskin in a field or in the woods some day. Snakes have no ears. Rattlesnakes catch food by using their eyes and pits. Pits are special holes that can sense when there is a warm animal nearby. There is a pit by each eye. Rattlesnakes eat mice, rats, rabbits and other small animals. They bite their prey and the animal dies in a few minutes. Long upper teeth called fangs are hollow so venom can flow through to the animal. When in danger rattlesnakes shake their tails. The rattle sound is a fast, clicking noise made by the bony rings on the rattlesnake's tail. This is a signal that a rattlesnake is frightened and may strike!

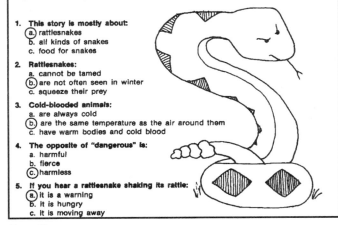

1. This story is mostly about:
   a. rattlesnakes
   b. all kinds of snakes
   c. food for snakes

2. Rattlesnakes:
   a. cannot be tamed
   b. are not often seen in winter
   c. squeeze their prey

3. Cold-blooded animals:
   a. are always cold
   b. are the same temperature as the air around them
   c. have warm bodies and cold blood

4. The opposite of "dangerous" is:
   a. harmful
   b. fierce
   c. harmless

5. If you hear a rattlesnake shaking its rattle:
   a. it is a warning
   b. it is hungry
   c. it is moving away

Page 30

Name

Sea Horses

The sea horse is actually a fish but it doesn't act like one. There are twenty-five different kinds of sea horses. The largest kind grows to be twelve inches. Most sea horses are three to six inches long. They have two skeletons—one on the outside of their bodies and the other on the inside. Hard plates cover the sea horse like a suit of armor. Sea horses are usually gray or black.

The sea horse uses his tail much like a monkey does. The tail is wrapped around plants or coral to anchor it in place. Sea horses often hide in the same place for hours. When a sea horse wants to go forward or backward it moves its dorsal fin. The dorsal fin is in the middle of its back. Small animals are sucked into the sea horse's snout-shaped mouth for food.

Male sea horses have a pouch like a kangaroo. This pouch is part of the interesting way sea horses breed and care for their young. Eggs are put in the male's pouch by the female. The father sea horse gets very heavy and can hardly swim from the weight of the babies in his pouch. The babies grow inside the pouch for forty-five days. Then almost two hundred baby sea horses wriggle out of the pouch and swim away. Babies are not taken care of by their parents. They swim away to sea plants and hang on with their tiny tails. Many are eaten by ocean creatures. At five months they are fully grown.

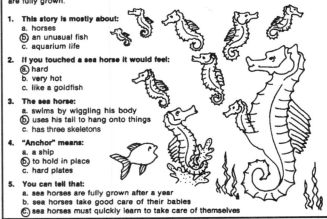

1. This story is mostly about:
   a. horses
   b. an unusual fish
   c. aquarium life

2. If you touched a sea horse it would feel:
   a. hard
   b. very hot
   c. like a goldfish

3. The sea horse:
   a. swims by wiggling his body
   b. uses his tail to hang onto things
   c. has three skeletons

4. "Anchor" means:
   a. a ship
   b. to hold in place
   c. hard plates

5. You can tell that:
   a. sea horses are fully grown after a year
   b. sea horses take good care of their babies
   c. sea horses must quickly learn to take care of themselves

Page 31

Name

Guinea Pigs

Guinea pigs are rodents. They are not related to pigs. Why they are called Guinea pigs is a mystery. Guinea pigs come in a variety of colors. Their hair can be short, long, curly or straight. Guinea pigs are born with their eyes open and with a full coat of fur. They look like miniature adult guinea pigs. They love to eat and play and spend the days sleeping.

A pet guinea pig will need a cage. You can buy cages of wire or plastic. Cardboard boxes will not work because the animal can gnaw its way out. Like most rodents, guinea pigs like to gnaw. Give them some clothespins, twigs or a piece of hard wood to chew on. Gnawing files down their teeth which are always growing. Without gnawing the teeth would get too long. You can buy guinea pig food at the pet store. They also like bits of fruit and vegetables.

A cardboard box can be put in the cage. The guinea pig will have a grand time climbing in and out of the box. They are fun to watch.

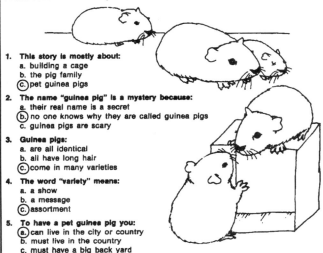

1. This story is mostly about:
   a. building a cage
   b. the pig family
   c. pet guinea pigs

2. The name "guinea pig" is a mystery because:
   a. their real name is a secret
   b. no one knows why they are called guinea pigs
   c. guinea pigs are scary

3. Guinea pigs:
   a. are all identical
   b. all have long hair
   c. come in many varieties

4. The word "variety" means:
   a. a show
   b. a message
   c. assortment

5. To have a pet guinea pig you:
   a. can live in the city or country
   b. must live in the country
   c. must have a big back yard

Page 32

Answer Key

Name _____

Mynah Birds

The colorful mynah bird has a shiny black body, yellow legs and feet, and a bright orange beak. This bird is about the size of a small chicken. Mynah birds are very interesting pets. They need a cage, fresh water, mynah bird food and some fresh fruits. Grapes are a special treat for a mynah bird. Adults are fed once a day. When buying a pet, get a bird that is as young as possible. They can be purchased at six weeks of age. Mynah birds live to be about fifteen years old.

Showing off is typical of mynah birds. They are fun to watch. The Mynah can imitate voices. The first words are the hardest for them to learn. Once they start talking, they will quickly learn to say more. You can teach your bird to talk by saying words over and over in the same voice. You must be patient and practice with the bird every day. Both the male and female mynah can learn to be good talkers. They can change the way they talk and imitate several different people. A dog or cat can also be imitated by the mynah bird.

On a warm day let your mynah bird take a bath. A bowl of lukewarm, shallow water makes a perfect bird bath. The mynah bird will put on quite a show when taking its bath. You will probably have as much fun watching as the bird will have in its bath!

1. A good title for this story is:
   a. A Talking Bird
   b. Bird Houses
   c. Song Birds

2. A mynah bird:
   a. learns to talk by listening to others
   b. can only speak English
   c. learns to talk by itself

3. The best way to teach your bird is:
   a. to teach it many different things at once
   b. to practice the same lesson every day
   c. to practice the same lesson weekly

4. The word "imitate" means:
   a. frighten
   b. copy
   c. listen

5. Mynah birds probably:
   a. do not understand the meaning of what they say
   b. are shy
   c. can make up things to say

Page 33

Name _____

Blue Whale

The blue whale is the largest animal that ever lived. It is as long as eight elephants standing in a row. This gigantic animal eats tiny plants and animals in the sea. Isn't it strange that the largest animal eats food that is so small? There are two kinds of whales. One side of the whale family has teeth, and the other branch of the family is the toothless whale. Blue whales do not have teeth. Their throats are small and they cannot swallow anything large. The blue whale scoops up a giant mouthful of water, closes its mouth and then strains the water back out into the sea. A brush-like strainer called a baleen lets the water go out but holds in plants and animals for the whale to swallow.

Whales are not fish. They are mammals just like you. Mammals breathe air, are warm-blooded, have hair and drink milk from their mothers. Whales can drown if held under water. Their hair is just a few bristles.

The blue whale is an endangered species. There is concern that the blue whale may soon disappear forever. Too many have been hunted and killed by man. Now there are laws to protect the whales.

1. The best title for this story is:
   a. The Biggest Animal Ever
   b. A Large Fish
   c. All About Mammals

2. The blue whale's enemy has been:
   a. killer whales
   b. large ships
   c. man

3. The whale family includes:
   a. fish, crab and lobsters
   b. toothed and toothless whales
   c. only whales without teeth

4. The word "endangered" means:
   a. in danger
   b. not in danger
   c. protected

5. Laws that protect whales:
   a. make sure there aren't too many whales
   b. let whales live and reproduce
   c. are silly—whales can protect themselves

Page 34

Name _____

Horses

Horses have helped people for many years. They pull carts, wagons, plows and carry people on their backs. Horses are beautiful, graceful animals. These powerful animals are gentle friends to people.

A horse needs a stable that is clean and dry. It needs some protection from extreme cold and heat. Horses need exercise. They eat hay and grain and drink lots of fresh water. Every day a horse needs grooming. Grooming includes brushing, combing and rubbing the shiny coat and cleaning its hoofs. It is important to remove small stones that may be caught in its hoofs. Horseshoes should be changed about once every six weeks. Horses are trained to obey their riders. When training a horse you must move slowly, talk quietly and not get upset. Your horse will understand that you are the boss and it will want to obey you. If you do not know how to ride you should get riding instructions. Busy streets are not good places to ride horses. Horses are frightened by sudden movements and noises and may bolt and run. Ride on trails or in open spaces where you can enjoy a view of the world from the strong back of a horse.

1. This story is mostly about:
   a. taming wild horses
   b. shoeing a horse
   c. caring for a horse

2. Horses:
   a. can make people's work easier
   b. have recently started helping people
   c. cannot do heavy work

3. Horses require:
   a. daily grooming
   b. new shoes yearly
   c. fresh meat to eat

4. The word "shiny" means the opposite of:
   a. glossy
   b. hairy
   c. dull

5. The horse:
   a. must be treated kindly
   b. will obey when shouted at
   c. must be trained by an adult

Page 35

Name _____

Mexico

Ana and Sergio are from Mexico, a warm country south of the United States. They have pet roosters, rabbits, goats, and a baby lamb. Mexican children, like children all over the world, love animals. Each year they have a special day called St. Anthony's Day when they take the pets to church to be blessed.

Sometimes the children go to village marketplaces to buy or trade products from their parent's farm. Other times they go to Mexico City where they shop in discount stores for bargains.

The people go to fiestas (parties) to celebrate holidays. They sing, dance and break piñatas (containers shaped like objects which are filled with candy, fruit and toys).

Some Mexican people still follow the old ways of life, but modern customs, schools, and houses are taking over. Mexico City is a center of education. Some Americans and Canadians study in Mexican universities.

The children play baseball and soccer. They watch bullfights and jai alai games.

Mexican people have given the world many beautiful works of art. In Mexico you might see pyramids like those in Egypt.

1. Mexico is a country just ___south___ of the United States.

2. The children in the story live on a ___farm___ in Mexico.

3. ___St. Anthony's Day___ is a special day for people to have their pets blessed.

4. A ___piñata___ is a container filled with treats for use at ___fiestas or parties___.

5. Children play ___baseball___ and ___soccer___ in Mexico.

6. You could take cool clothes and sandals if you visit Mexico because ___it is warm there___ .

Individual Activities

1. Ask your teacher if you can weave, sing some Mexican songs or learn a Mexican dance. Draw a picture of a bookmark you could weave.

2. Read more about Mexico. Choose one subject to tell about in class.

Page 36

113

Answer Key

Name _____

Japan

Kentaro was born in Japan. Japan is a country made up of four large islands and many small ones. It is located in the Pacific Ocean near China.

Kentaro lives in Tokyo, which is a large city. He lives in a huge apartment building. Kentaro usually wears clothes like yours. On special days his sister dresses in a long robe called a kimono, which is tied around the waist with a sash called an obi. At school Kentaro learns a special kind of writing done with a brush. He enjoys judo, but baseball is his favorite sport.

Kentaro likes to look at the cherry trees in bloom and enjoys special holidays like the Boys' Festival. His sister's favorite holiday is Girls' Day, the Festival of Dolls. His mother and her friends enjoy making beautiful flower arrangements. Kentaro thinks of Japan as a land of many mountains. One of the most famous mountains in the world is Japan's Mt. Fuji.

Kentaro likes to eat tacos and pizza now, but he still enjoys dishes made with rice, the main food in Japan.

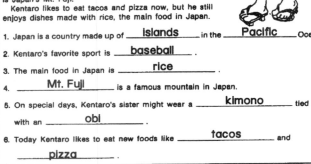

1. Japan is a country made up of __islands__ in the __Pacific__ Ocean.
2. Kentaro's favorite sport is __baseball__.
3. The main food in Japan is __rice__.
4. __Mt. Fuji__ is a famous mountain in Japan.
5. On special days, Kentaro's sister might wear a __kimono__ tied with an __obi__.
6. Today Kentaro likes to eat new foods like __tacos__ and __pizza__.

Individual Activities

1. Read more about Japan. (You should choose one topic such as food, products, minerals, etc.) Locate the country on the map and tell your class some of the things you have learned.
2. Write a story about a day in Kentaro's life in Japan.

Page 37

Name _____

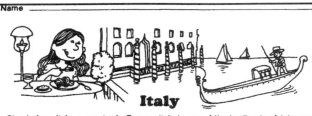

Canada

Gordon is from Canada, the second largest country in the world. It is made up of provinces that are somewhat like states. Most of the Canadian people live within 200 miles of the U.S. border, because much of northern Canada is wilderness and **wasteland** (land that is not very useful for living on or for growing things).

Canada is a scenic land that attracts many tourists and has many natural resources which make it valuable for mining, fishing, forestry and manufacturing. It is one of the most successful countries in the world. Though it is an independent country, the King or Queen of Great Britain is also King or Queen of Canada. Since Canada shares common interests and backgrounds with the U.S., the two countries have been good friends for many years.

Hockey, baseball and football are popular sports in both countries. Being in Canada is somewhat like being in the United States, England, and France all at once, since the land was settled by the English and French. Both languages are spoken there.

1. Canada is a country similar to the U.S. that is made up of __provinces__.
2. __Hockey__, __baseball__, and __football__ are popular sports in Canada.
3. Canada is a very __scenic__ land.
4. Most of the people live close to the __U.S. border__.
5. Land that is not useful to man may be called __wasteland__.
6. Canadian customs are somewhat similar to customs in __England__, __France__ and __the U.S.__.

Individual Activities

1. Use a travel folder or the encyclopedia to help you make a notebook of places to see in Canada.
2. Read about Quebec and see if you can see likenesses and differences between it and the rest of Canada.

Page 38

Name _____

Puerto Rico

Juan is from Puerto Rico, an island southwest of Florida. Puerto Rico means "rich port." The climate, its most important natural resource, brings visitors and allows a variety of crops to grow. There are many modern hotels there. People enjoy deep sea fishing and skin diving in this area.

Puerto Ricans are United States citizens and can move to the U.S. without permission. Perhaps by the time you read this Puerto Ricans may have decided to make their territory another state.

It is believed that Columbus discovered and landed on this island while sailing for Spain. The U.S. acquired Puerto Rico from Spain in 1898. Many people speak Spanish and celebrate with colorful festivals. Spanish music and art are popular. The U.S. government set up a public school system in Puerto Rico.

1. Puerto Rico is an island near __Florida__, U.S.A.
2. Many hotels are needed because Puerto Rico has many __tourists or visitors__.
3. Puerto Ricans can move to the U.S. without special permission because they are __U.S. citizens__.
4. Many customs of Puerto Rico are __Spanish__, because the area was discovered by Columbus for __Spain__.
5. Another word for weather throughout the year is __climate__.
6. Tourists probably choose Puerto Rico for a vacation because of the excellent __weather or climate__.

Individual Activities

1. Ask a travel agent for a pamphlet about Puerto Rico. Plan a pretend trip to the island. Tell how you would travel, what kind of clothes you would take, and what you would do there.
2. Draw a map of Puerto Rico. Show some important cities.

Page 39

Name _____

Italy

Gina is from Italy, a country in Europe. Italy is one of the leading **tourist** (person making a tour or pleasure trip) centers of the world. Each year people travel to Italy to visit Roman ruins, monuments, beautiful churches, art museums and opera houses. The Leaning Tower of Pisa is one of the most famous tourist attractions in the world. Vatican City, home of the Pope and center of the Catholic Church, is another popular spot for visitors.

Vacationers may choose to spend time on the sunny beaches or travel to ski resorts in the Alps. They can enjoy gliding down the **canals** (waterways) of Venice in special boats called gondolas.

Gina loves to eat **pasta** (food made from a flour and water mixture) such as spaghetti or noodles. You would probably enjoy having dinner with her.

1. Italy is located in __Europe__.
2. The __Leaning Tower of Pisa__ is a famous tourist attraction.
3. People who visit another area for pleasure (fun) are called __tourists__.
4. You might enjoy riding in a special kind of boat called a __gondola__.
5. Five places where a visitor could learn about Italian history are __ruins__, __monuments__, __churches__, __art museums__, or __opera houses__.
6. Two opposite types of places you might choose for vacations in Italy are __beaches__ and __ski resorts__.

Individual Activities

1. Locate Pisa, Tower of, in an encyclopedia. Tell your class why it is leaning.
2. Read about a famous Italian artist such as Michaelangelo, da Vinci or Raphael. Write a report to share with your class.

Page 40

Name _____

Norway and Sweden

Kari and Sven's mother is from Norway, while their father is from Sweden. Both countries are in a part of northern Europe called Scandinavia. Part of each country is above the Arctic Circle. These countries are called "lands of the midnight sun" because during part of the summer the sun shines 24 hours a day. The area also has much snow, and skiing is a national sport. If you lived there you would probably learn to ski before you begin school.

The people of Norway do a lot of fishing and shipping. There are many long, narrow inlets where the sea reaches into the land called fjords. The land is high and rocky with little farmland. Rivers rushing down the mountainside provide cheap electricity for manufacturing. There are many famous writers, artists and musicians such as Edvard Grieg who came from this land.

Sweden is one of the most **prosperous** (successful) countries in the world. One famous way of serving meals is called the smörgasbörd, where a variety of cold and hot foods are put out for people to choose from. Perhaps you have been to a smörgasbörd. In school the children study subjects as you do, but everyone is also taught gymnastics. Many Americans buy Scandinavian furniture. Santa Lucia Day is a favorite holiday which reminds the people that Christmas is coming.

1. Two similar countries in Scandinavia are __Norway__ and __Sweden__ .

2. If you wanted to choose from a variety of foods you might go to a __smörgasbörd__ .

3. Fjords are common in __Norway__ .

4. Many Americans buy Scandinavian __furniture__ .

5. A word that means successful is __prosperous__ .

6. Since the sun shines all day and night during the summer, these countries have been nicknamed __lands of the midnight sun__ .

Individual Activities

1. Use the encyclopedia to find out more about fjords. Then draw or paint a picture of a scene in Norway or Sweden.
2. Find out more about Edvard Grieg. See if you can get a record with some of his music to play for the class.

Page 41

Name _____

India

Seeta is a girl from India. India has more people than any other country except China, its northern neighbor. It is a land of **contrasts** including deserts, jungles, plains, mountains and lowlands. There are three seasons—hot, cold and rainy. The people are of many races and religions and speak about 180 languages. Some people wear ancient costumes, while others wear western clothes as you do. Sometimes people wear suits to work but change to traditional, loose clothing at home. Cloth wrapped around the head is called a turban. Women often wear a straight piece of cloth draped around the body as a long dress. This is called a sari.

India has large cities that are business and educational centers. It also has many small villages with mud and straw homes and very small schools.

Music is played on instruments somewhat like guitars but with more strings. Their music sounds different to us because they play complicated melodies instead of chords. Dancers tell stories with their hands and fingers. Beautiful carvings are made from stone and ivory.

1. India is a country of many people and a land of __contrasts__ .

2. Some people prefer both the __new__ and __old__ ways of life.

3. Stories are told by dancers using their __hands__ and __fingers__ .

4. A cloth wrapped around the head is called a __turban__ , while one draped around the body like a dress is called a __sari__ .

5. In the story, the word "contrasts" means __differences__ .

6. Because of the many different languages spoken it might be hard for some Indian people to __understand__ each other.

Individual Activities

1. Use an encyclopedia to find a map showing the products of India. Make a product map to share with your class.
2. See if your public library has any recordings of Indian music. Play the records for for your class.

Page 42

Name _____

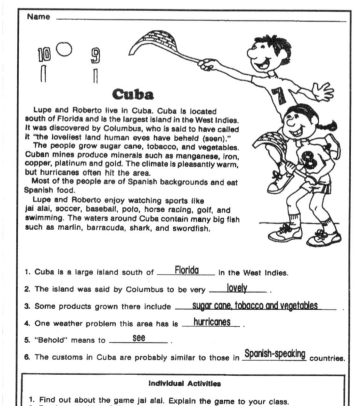

Cuba

Lupe and Roberto live in Cuba. Cuba is located south of Florida and is the largest island in the West Indies. It was discovered by Columbus, who is said to have called it "the loveliest land human eyes have beheld (seen)."

The people grow sugar cane, tobacco, and vegetables. Cuban mines produce minerals such as manganese, iron, copper, platinum and gold. The climate is pleasantly warm, but hurricanes often hit the area.

Most of the people are of Spanish backgrounds and eat Spanish food.

Lupe and Roberto enjoy watching sports like jai alai, soccer, baseball, polo, horse racing, golf, and swimming. The waters around Cuba contain many big fish such as marlin, barracuda, shark, and swordfish.

1. Cuba is a large island south of __Florida__ in the West Indies.

2. The island was said by Columbus to be very __lovely__ .

3. Some products grown there include __sugar cane, tobacco and vegetables__ .

4. One weather problem this area has is __hurricanes__ .

5. "Behold" means to __see__ .

6. The customs in Cuba are probably similar to those in __Spanish-speaking__ countries.

Individual Activities

1. Find out about the game jai alai. Explain the game to your class.
2. Read more about Cuba today. How has it changed?

Page 43

Name _____

Israel

Moishe grew up in Israel, a country in the Middle East. Most of the mountains, rivers and cities still have the same names they had in Biblical times. The Jewish people returned to this land in 1948 and have worked hard to build a modern nation. They lost their land many years ago. All Jewish people are welcome to move to Israel.

The Israelis celebrate most of the same holidays that Jewish children everywhere celebrate. They also have tree-planting ceremonies where you may have a tree planted in memory of someone you knew.

The people speak Hebrew or Arabic, and some English. Although Israel is in the Middle East, the cities and towns seem more like western cities in North America or Europe.

The people of Israel eat mostly bread, grains, fruit and dairy products. Many of the people work in manufacturing or farming. Often families and friends work together and share the profits on one large farm known as a kibbutz. Each person has his or her special job. Some do the farming while others care for the children or do different work.

1. Although the __Jewish__ people were once sent out of Israel, they have come back to build their nation.

2. Israelis probably eat __less__ (more, less) meat than we do.

3. To honor someone you may __plant a tree__ in Israel.

4. Three languages spoken in Israel are __Hebrew, Arabic and English__ .

5. A farm shared by several families or people is called a __kibbutz__ .

6. The Jewish people probably were willing to fight and work hard because they wanted __a land of their own__ .

Individual Activities

1. In an encyclopedia find the Israeli flag. Draw a picture of it. Tell your class what the colors and symbols stand for.
2. Watch the newspaper for articles telling about Israel today. Share one article with your class.

Page 44

Answer Key

Name _____

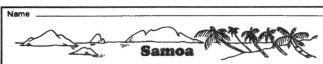

Samoa

Saru's parents came from the island of Samoa in the Pacific Ocean about five thousand miles southwest of California. Most of the islands in that area were formed by volcanoes and are surrounded by coral reefs.

The climate is pleasant, except for periods between January and March when gales and hurricanes sweep in.

The people sell copra (the meat of coconuts), cacao, and bananas to other countries. Sending products to other countries is called "exporting."

The people are Polynesians as are the Hawaiian people. "Polynesia" means "many islands." Some people of Samoa carry on ancient ways and crafts. They may dress in colorful costumes and paint their faces. They do fascinating island dances. In Hawaii you can visit the Polynesian Cultural Center and see sample homes that show you how the Samoan people live. You may also see a Polynesian dancing show. The people are graceful, athletic, and love water sports such as swimming, diving and surfing. Saru wears a simple cloth wrapped around his body from his waist to his ankles. It is called a lavalava. The people still make tapa cloth by beating the bark of paper mulberry trees. It is used for clothing and decorating houses.

1. Another name for the Pacific islands is ___Polynesia___ .

2. It might be hard to reach some of the islands because they are surrounded by _____
___coral reefs___ .

3. In their spare time the people enjoy ___water sports___

4. Polynesians make tapa cloth from ___paper mulberry trees___

5. ___Export___ means to send products to other countries for sale or trade.

6. January through March would not be the best time to visit Samoa because of
___hurricanes___ and ___gales___ .

Individual Activities
1. Look up "coral reef." Tell your class what you learned.
2. Borrow the book "The Cay" from a library. If it is too hard for you to read, have a parent or your teacher read it to you or the class.

Page 45

Name _____

Brazil

Rosa is from Brazil, the largest country in South America. Her country supplies the world with such products as coffee, sugar cane, minerals, lumber, cattle, hogs, cotton, and cacao beans from which we make chocolate and cocoa. Much of the country's trade is done with the United States. It is a modern country. Most of the people live near the Atlantic Ocean.

The majority of people speak Portuguese, since Portugal received the land from Spain in 1494. Soccer, the favorite sport in Brazil, is becoming a favorite in North America too. Pelé, a famous player from Brazil, also played in the United States.

Rosa wears a white blouse and dark skirt to school, much as students do in some schools in other countries. When school is not in session she loves to go to the beach. Sometimes Rosa and other Brazilians prefer to sleep in hammocks which are made of cloth or straw and are hung by the ends from walls or posts. Modern hotels may offer hammocks instead of beds.

There are many offices and hotels. They are often decorated with bright colored tiles. Artists there are now painting very modern designs.

The great Amazon River winds through the jungles of Brazil. This river has more water than any other river. Big game hunters search the area for jaguars, mountain lions and crocodiles. You may have seen this jungle area in movies or television.

1. Brazil is the ___largest___ country in South America and supplies the world with many ___products___ .

2. The chocolate you eat probably began as ___cacao___ beans.

3. The favorite sport is ___soccer___ .

4. The ___Amazon___ is an extremely large and important river.

5. A lounge or bed hung from the ends is called a ___hammock___ .

6. Before the people spoke Portuguese, the language in Brazil was probably
___Spanish___

Individual Activities
1. Begin a flag book. Draw the flag of Brazil for your book.
2. Write a short story or play about a trip to Brazil. How would you get there? What would you see and do? Use ideas from the story, encyclopedia, or travel folders.

Page 46

Name _____

Peru

Alma is from Peru in South America. Peru is on the Pacific Ocean side of South America and is about three times as big as California. Alma is looking forward to Independence Day which is in July. There will be parades, music, fireworks and a special family dinner with duckling and rice.

Alma's parents have a small farm in the valley. Her grandparents live high in the mountains and herd cattle, sheep and llamas. Their home is made of adobe (sun dried clay bricks) and has a red tile roof. They have a red tile roof. They have less furniture than most Americans have in their homes. When school is over Alma loves to jump rope.

The clothes worn in Peru near the coast may be much like yours. In the mountains they wear woolen clothing. A blanket-like covering with a hole in the middle is worn over other clothes to keep warm. It is called a poncho.

Peru was once the land of the Inca Indians. Parts of ancient Inca cities are still in the mountains of Peru. Later Spanish soldiers conquered the country. Peruvians may have both Indian and Spanish ancestors.

The mountains of Peru are rich in minerals including copper, gold, silver, iron, lead and zinc. Perhaps you have some jewelry made of silver from Peru.

1. Peru is a large country in ___South America___ near the ___Pacific___ Ocean.

2. If you wanted to visit Inca cities, you would probably go to the ___mountains___ of Peru.

3. Some minerals we might get from Peru are ___(accept any from story)___ .

4. For cold weather, children and adults can put on their ___ponchos___

5. Sun dried clay is called ___adobe___ .

6. Since the country had many Indians and Spanish, it is likely most people can speak either ___Spanish___ or ___an Indian language___ .

Individual Activities
1. Look for llama in the dictionary. Draw a llama.
2. Read about the Inca Indians. Write a report and tell your class what you learned.

Page 47

Name _____

女 媽 心 **China** 姐 妹
woman   mother   heart   elder sister   younger sister

Mei Ling's family is from China. It is near Russia, India and Japan. China has the largest population of any country in the world. Most people are farmers who grow China's food supply. Rice is the main food. Rice dishes made with pork or chicken are favorites. They irrigate their fields by bringing water from streams or rivers.

The Chinese people were the first to develop gunpowder, paper, porcelain, printing and silk cloth.

Though many people live in villages, new city areas have modern offices, factories, stores and apartments.

Chinese art began before history was written. The ancient Chinese made beautiful carved jade and stone, bronze statues, porcelain ware, painted scrolls, etc.

In school, children may learn to read and write the interesting Chinese symbols with a brush. The children love to celebrate the Chinese New Year. They celebrate all night and welcome the New Year with fireworks. They may receive gifts and coins.

1. China has more ___people___ than any other country.

2. Chinese people were the first to develop such things as ___gunpowder___ , ___paper___ , ___printing___ , ___porcelain___ and ___silk cloth___ .

3. Most people earn a living by ___farming___ .

4. ___Rice___ is the main food and can be made into a special dish by adding ___pork___ or ___chicken___

5. To bring water to an area for farming is called ___irrigation___ .

6. The more people a country has, the more ___food___ it must grow or get in trade from other countries.

Individual Activities
1. Find pictures of Chinese art work in a book or encyclopedia. Sketch some of them or make a Chinese type painting of your own.
2. Ask your teacher if he or she can invite someone to talk about China, or find an article about China today in the newspaper and tell your class what you have learned.

Page 48

116

Answer Key

Egypt

Hassan and Zainab are from Egypt, a country that borders on the Mediterranean and Red Seas. Since Egypt is mainly a desert area, the people depend on the Nile River which provides most of the water and rich soil. The River is a natural resource (something in nature that is helpful to man).

Often children help their parents with farm work. They go to school to learn to read and write their language. Some children learn to make bronze objects or food items such as butter and cheese. They enjoy hopscotch and games like marbles, played with pebbles.

Long ago huge pyramids were built in Egypt as tombs, or burial places, for dead kings. Many beautiful things were found in tombs like that of King Tut.

1. Egyptians depend strongly on the __Nile River__
2. Tombs are special places for people who are __dead__
3. The Nile River provides both __water__ and __rich soil__.
4. The children use pebbles to play a game like __marbles__
5. A __natural resource__ is something provided by nature that is useful to man.
6. A good place for a farm in Egypt would be near the __Nile River__

Individual Activities

1. Read about Egyptian art or the King Tut Treasures. Make some sketches of their art objects or paintings.
2. Use an encyclopedia to find out what products are produced in Egypt. What product do the Arab countries have that Egypt and so many countries need?

Page 49

Panama

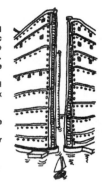

Miguel is from Panama. Panama is located in Central America, just north of South America. Years ago the United States built a waterway between the Pacific and Atlantic Oceans called the Panama Canal. Now ships do not have to travel all the way around South America to carry goods. The United States Congress voted to give the canal to the Panamanian people.

The climate in Panama is generally hot with a great deal of rain. Most of the people speak Spanish, but many speak English as you do.

Rice, corn, and beans are the main foods eaten in Panama. Miguel's mother grinds the corn and makes paste for tortillas.

The people wear lightweight clothes much like you wear in warm weather. On special days the people have celebrations called fiestas, and the women wear long dresses with beautiful embroidery. The men wear loose embroidered shirts.

1. Panama is located in __Central America__ which is between North America and __South America__
2. A canal is a __waterway__ between two places.
3. Most people in Panama speak __Spanish__, though many speak __English__.
4. The Panama Canal is important because it connects the __Pacific__ and __Atlantic__ Oceans.
5. A food made from ground corn is a __tortilla__.
6. Panamanians wear lightweight clothing because __their weather is warm__

Individual Activities

1. Read about the Panama Canal. Draw a map showing its location. Tell why it is so important.
2. Watch the newspaper for articles about Panama and the Canal.

Page 50

Great Britain

Anne and Alan live in Great Britain. Great Britain includes England, Scotland, Wales and Northern Ireland. In England you can visit London and see the famous tower clock, Big Ben. You might go on a fox hunt, and of course you would stay for afternoon tea. In Northern Ireland you would view the beautiful green countryside that gives the country the nickname "Emerald Isle." You might listen to a storyteller telling folktales about fairies or leprechauns. In Scotland you could visit a clan gathering where a group of related families gather for fun. Some of the men would be wearing kilts, which are skirt-like garments made of the special clan plaid. They play the bagpipes and do a country dance such as the Highland Fling.

1. Great Britain includes __England__, __Scotland__, __Wales__ and __Northern Ireland__
2. In London you could see a tower clock called __Big Ben__
3. In the afternoon the English drink __tea__
4. In Scotland they play an instrument called a __bagpipe__
5. You might visit a clan gathering in __Scotland__
6. "Emerald Isle" is another name for __Ireland__

Individual Activities

1. Have your classmates find out where their ancestors lived. Mark these countries on a world map with the classmate's name.
2. Read and tell or write about the native country of one of your ancestors. Make a display of the reports for Open House.

Page 51

Nigeria

Kehinde is from Nigeria in Western Africa, a country of many people and unusual animals. It is a land of contrasts (big differences) with very rainy areas as well as hot dry areas. Nigeria has the largest population in Africa.

Many languages are spoken in Nigeria including English, which is taught in most schools. The government is working to develop the natural resources and to improve schools. It is one of Africa's largest oil producers.

Nigerians produce many crops. Plows and oxen are often used instead of modern farm machinery. Some people are nomads who move from place to place. They live mainly in desert areas herding camels, goats and sheep. They may live in tents or homes made of branches and plants. Some families live and work together in groups called tribes, sharing old ways.

New apartments and office buildings make the big cities much like ours. The people may dress as we do, or they may wear long flowing robes. Women sometimes cover their faces with veils. People in very hot areas wear little clothing.

Many famous legends and folktales come from this land. Its music has a powerful beat of drums.

1. Nigeria is a land of __contrasts__ with rainy and __dry__ areas.
2. Nigeria has the __largest__ population in Africa.
3. Nigeria is one of Africa's largest producers of __oil__
4. Nomads are people who __move__ from place to place.
5. People who live and work together in groups are called __tribes__
6. Two other names for stories are __legends__ and __folktales__

Individual Activities

1. Read about the plants and animals of this area. Plan a pretend trip to Africa. Perhaps it will be a safari. Draw pictures of what you will see.
2. Read an African folktale to your class. Perhaps your library has records with African folktales or legends you can share.

Page 52

Answer Key

Name

American Indian—Navajo

Sam's ancestors were the first Americans. These people are called Indians, because Columbus thought he had reached India. There are many different tribes of Indians who live in different ways.

Sam's tribe, the Navajo, lives in the southwestern United States. It is believed that they came to Arizona and New Mexico from Canada. The Pueblo Indians taught the Navajo to grow corn, weave, and make sand paintings. Many Navajo artists paint murals and water colors. Beautiful designs are used for jewelry, pottery, weaving, and clothing.

Some Navajo Indians prefer to follow the old ways. Most of them live, at least part of the time, on land set aside by the government called reservations. Many people work there, farming, raising cattle, doing craft work, etc. Others may work in nearby factories, mines or at professions such as teaching or medicine.

1. The Indian originally received that name from __Columbus__ who believed he had

   reached _____India_____ .

2. Indians today may still live on _____reservations_____ if they wish to do so.

3. A reservation is an area of _____land set aside for Indians_____ .

4. The __Navajo__ Indians live in the __southwestern__ United States.

5. Beautiful Navajo designs are used today in __jewelry__ , __weaving__ ,

   __pottery__ and __clothing__ , etc.

6. Some Indian tribes taught other tribes much as the Indians taught white settlers. The

   Pueblo Indians taught the Navajo Indians to __grow corn__ , __weave__ and

   make __sand paintings__

Individual Activities
1. Find a copy of a poem about Indians such as "Hiawatha" by Longfellow. Practice reading the poem aloud. Read it to your class.
2. Locate **Indians** in your encyclopedia. Get ideas about Indian designs. Try drawing the designs on paper or clay.

Page 53

Name

Vietnam

Kim is from Vietnam. The country is near China. The people of Kim's country have similarities to the people of China or Japan. Both countries had a great influence on Vietnam. Many people are rice farmers and live in small villages near river deltas. Rice is the main crop. More people now live in cities. They are businessmen, shopkeepers, or merchants.

The people value education and are training skilled workers. They are encouraging people to attend universities.

There are many forests in Vietnam. A variety of minerals can be found in this country. Rice and rubber are important exports.

1. Vietnam is similar to _____China_____ and _____Japan_____ .

2. Some of the people live in _____small villages_____ near __river deltas__ .

3. Some important products exported from Vietnam are _____rice_____

   and __rubber__ .

4. Farmers may still use __simple wooden plows (or tools)__ .

5. Vietnam is encouraging more people to attend __universities__ .

6. People who live in the cities might be __businessmen__ ,

   __shopkeepers__ or __merchants__ .

Individual Activities
1. See if anyone in your class has relatives from this country. Invite those persons to give a talk about the country. Encourage people from different countries to visit your classroom to talk about their land of birth.
2. Look at a map of Vietnam. Draw an outline of the country.

Page 54

Name ___ Date ___

Wonder Woman

Some sports writers thought Babe **Didrikson** was the best **athlete** that ever lived. Babe Didrikson could play almost any sport well. She played basketball, baseball, football, and tennis. She also swam, bowled and even did some boxing.

Babe Didrikson played on the All-America women's basketball team in 1931 and 1932. She often scored 30 points or more in a game. Babe also won two gold medals in track and set world records at the Olympics. She loved playing any sport but became most famous as a golfer.

Babe began playing golf in the late 1930's. She set a record by winning seventeen women's golf matches in a row. She was the first American woman to win the British Women's golf match. She won 82 matches in all.

In 1954, Babe Didrikson was named the best woman in sports from 1900 to 1950.

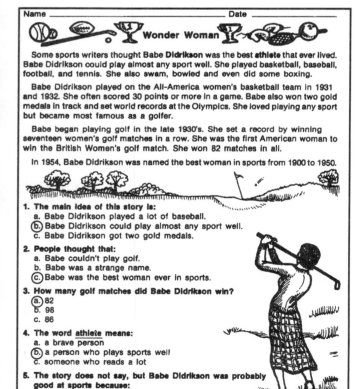

1. The main idea of this story is:
   a. Babe Didrikson played a lot of baseball.
   ⓑ Babe Didrikson could play almost any sport well.
   c. Babe Didrikson got two gold medals.

2. People thought that:
   a. Babe couldn't play golf.
   b. Babe was a strange name.
   ⓒ Babe was the best woman ever in sports.

3. How many golf matches did Babe Didrikson win?
   ⓐ 82
   b. 98
   c. 86

4. The word **athlete** means:
   a. a brave person
   ⓑ a person who plays sports well
   c. someone who reads a lot

5. The story does not say, but Babe Didrikson was probably good at sports because:
   a. She studied math.
   b. She ran every day.
   ⓒ She was very strong.

Page 55

Name ___ Date ___

Ten-Fingered Wizard

As a child José **Feliciano** listened to the radio. Music became his whole world. José was born blind and could not do a lot of things other children could do. While other children were playing outside, José learned to play the guitar and sing. He also learned to play the banjo, conga drums, harmonica, piano and organ. He couldn't read music so he learned to play by ear.

José began performing on the guitar for people when he was seventeen. One man called José a "ten-fingered wizard". His first big record was "Light My Fire". He won many awards for his songs. José wrote the title song for the television series, "Chico and the Man". That song also became popular.

Today José Feliciano performs all over the world. His blindness doesn't stop him from doing things anymore. He has learned to swim, sail a boat, play baseball and ride bicycles.

1. The main idea of this story is:
   a. José Feliciano owns a radio.
   b. José Feliciano is an actor.
   ⓒ José Feliciano plays the guitar well.

2. José Feliciano:
   ⓐ can play many different instruments
   b. lives in England
   c. enjoys skydiving

3. One of José Feliciano's big record hits was:
   a. Ten-Fingered Wizard
   ⓑ Light My Fire
   c. All Over the World

4. To **play by ear** means:
   a. to put your ear on a piano
   b. to make music with your ears
   ⓒ to hear music and be able to play it

5. Being blind and learning to play an instrument is probably:
   ⓐ very hard
   b. very easy
   c. done by many people

Page 56

Answer Key

Pioneer Girl

Laura Ingalls Wilder was born in a log cabin on the edge of the Big Woods of **Wisconsin** in 1867. When she was still a baby, the family traveled West by covered wagon. Laura grew up on the prairie and went to school in a one-room schoolhouse. She became a teacher when she was sixteen and later married Almanzo Wilder.

Laura Wilder wrote about her life in the "Little House" books. Each book told about the sadness and joys of pioneer life. "Little House in the Big Woods" told about her childhood. "Farmer Boy" is the story of Almanzo Wilder's childhood. "These Happy Golden Years" describes the first years of Laura and Almanzo's marriage and the birth of their daughter Rose.

Laura Wilder received many prizes for her books. The "Little House" books were so popular, they were made into a television series.

Laura Wilder lived on a farm in **Missouri** until her death in 1957. She was 90 years old.

1. The main idea of this story is:
   a. Laura lived in a log cabin.
   b. **Laura wrote books about her life.**
   c. Laura lived to be 90 years old.

2. Laura's school was:
   a. painted white
   b. very large
   c. **very small**

3. Laura's family were:
   a. bankers
   b. sailors
   c. **pioneers**

4. The word **describes** means:
   a. **tells about**
   b. becomes sad
   c. runs around

5. Since Laura Wilder lived a long time:
   a. She traveled around the world.
   b. She met the president.
   c. **She saw many changes in the world.**

Page 57

The Sad-Faced Clown

He wore ragged clothes and always looked like he was just about to cry. Yet "Weary Willie" made children laugh for over 40 years. The man behind Weary Willie's clown face was Emmett Kelly. Emmett joined the circus in 1933 and soon after became a clown.

Emmett decided he wanted to be a very special clown. He didn't want to wear white face make-up. So Emmett invented the character "Weary Willie". Emmett made up his face with a dark beard and a large pink nose. He also drew a large turned-down mouth on his face. He dressed as a hobo in old, torn clothes.

The character Weary Willie never talked. Sometimes he pretended to sweep the circus ring with a broom. He tried to sweep away the spotlight, but it kept moving away from him. Other times, he tried to crack a peanut with an ax. Emmett performed with the Ringling Brothers, Barnum and Bailey Circus. His son, Emmett Kelly, Jr., also became a clown.

1. The main idea of this story is:
   a. Emmett Kelly was a sad man.
   b. Emmett Kelly drew pictures.
   c. **Emmett Kelly was a clown.**

2. Most clowns wear:
   a. **white face make-up**
   b. ragged clothes
   c. sad faces

3. As a clown, Emmett called himself:
   a. Sad Sack
   b. Weepy Walter
   c. **Weary Willie**

4. A **spotlight** is:
   a. a light that has spots on it
   b. **a light that moves and shines on one thing**
   c. a light spot on your clothes

5. People love clowns because:
   a. **They do funny things.**
   b. They all live in Boston.
   c. They are good swimmers.

Page 58

Finding a Cure

In the 1950's, polio was a dangerous illness. Every year many people became crippled or died because of polio. Then in 1953, Dr. Jonas Salk said he had found a cure. His medicine was made in the form of a **vaccine**. The vaccine was given by a shot. First Salk and his family took the medicine. The vaccine was found to be safe. Then almost two million school children were given polio shots in 1954. Soon people were not afraid of getting polio anymore.

In 1960, Dr. Albert Sabin made a stronger polio vaccine. He put it on sugar cubes. People didn't have to take polio shots anymore. They could eat their medicine. The Sabin vaccine lasted longer than the Salk vaccine. Thanks to these two men, polio has almost disappeared.

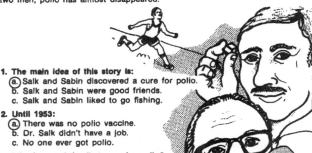

1. The main idea of this story is:
   a. **Salk and Sabin discovered a cure for polio.**
   b. Salk and Sabin were good friends.
   c. Salk and Sabin liked to go fishing.

2. Until 1953:
   a. **There was no polio vaccine.**
   b. Dr. Salk didn't have a job.
   c. No one ever got polio.

3. Who invented the first cure for polio?
   a. Sabin
   b. the Marx Brothers
   c. **Salk**

4. What is a **vaccine**?
   a. food
   b. **medicine**
   c. a soft drink

5. If Salk and Sabin had not found a cure for polio:
   a. **Many people would still get sick from polio.**
   b. People would not like them.
   c. Salk and Sabin would have bought a restaurant.

Page 59

Beatles Forever

The Beatles were probably the most popular group in rock music history. They changed rock music by using pretty tunes and interesting words. They also brought long hair into fashion. Because of their hair, they were also called the "mop tops". George Harrison, John Lennon, Paul McCartney and Ringo Starr were all born in Liverpool, England. They began performing in the early 60's. In 1962, they made their first record and by 1964, they had become world-famous. Some of their early hits were "Please, Please Me", and "I Wanna Hold Your Hand".

The Beatles toured the United States several times. They were greeted everywhere by fans who loved them and their music. The Beatles starred in two movies, "A Hard Day's Night" and "Help!"

The group broke up in 1970, but by that time they had sold more records than any other performers in popular music.

1. The main idea of this story is:
   a. **The Beatles were a very popular music group.**
   b. The Beatles made movies.
   c. The Beatles were born in Liverpool.

2. The Beatles were called the "mop tops" because:
   a. They carried mops and tops.
   b. They were very neat.
   c. **They had long hair.**

3. What kind of music did the Beatles play?
   a. jazz
   b. **rock**
   c. country western

4. The word **famous** means:
   a. funny
   b. **well-known**
   c. smart

5. You can tell that the Beatles' movies were probably:
   a. silly
   b. long
   c. **popular**

Page 60

FS-32046 Reading

Answer Key

Name _____ Date _____

Seeing in the Dark

When Anne Sullivan first met Helen Keller, Helen acted more like a wild animal than a child. At age two, before she learned to talk, Helen became very ill. The illness destroyed her sight and hearing. Helen never learned to talk. She could only make angry sounds or happy sounds. But Anne Sullivan was a very good teacher. After much hard work, she taught Helen to talk through sign language. Later, Helen learned to read and write **Braille**, the written language of the blind. Finally, when she was sixteen, Helen learned to speak.

Helen went to college. After finishing school, she began working to help the blind and the deaf-blind. She gave lectures, wrote books and visited the President of the United States. During World War II, she worked with soldiers who had been blinded in the war.

The motion picture, "The **Miracle** Worker", is based on Helen Keller's early life.

1. **The main idea of this story is:**
   a. Anne Sullivan was a good teacher.
   b. Helen liked college.
   c. Helen learned to overcome her problems. ✓
2. **Until she was sixteen, Helen:**
   a. did not go to school
   b. could not talk ✓
   c. did not eat spinach
3. **Helen learned to read:**
   a. Braille ✓
   b. Morse Code
   c. print
4. **What does destroyed mean?**
   a. to find
   b. to freeze
   c. to ruin ✓
5. **Helen probably wanted to help the blind because:**
   a. She thought it was interesting.
   b. She was blind herself. ✓
   c. She liked hard work.

Page 61

Name _____ Date _____

Square People

Some of the figures he drew had two noses, crossed eyes and twisted bodies. Yet Pablo **Picasso** is thought to be one of the most important artists of this century.

Picasso was born in Spain, but lived in France from 1904 until his death. His early drawings were simple. People looked like people and trees looked like trees. But soon Picasso began to experiment with his art. For a time he only used the color blue in his paintings. Then he began drawing figures that looked more like squares and triangles than people. He used dark colors and printed words in his paintings.

In 1937, The town **Guenerica** was destroyed in the Spanish Civil War. Picasso painted a picture called "Guenerica" as a protest against the war. It became his most famous painting.

Picasso's later paintings were easier to understand. Today his paintings hang in almost every large museum in the world.

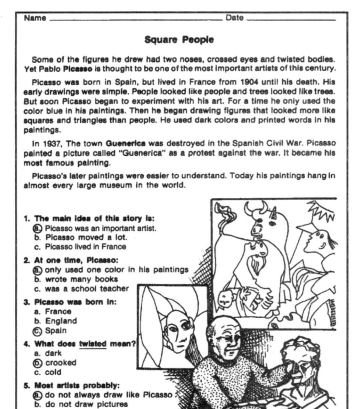

1. **The main idea of this story is:**
   a. Picasso was an important artist. ✓
   b. Picasso moved a lot.
   c. Picasso lived in France
2. **At one time, Picasso:**
   a. only used one color in his paintings ✓
   b. wrote many books
   c. was a school teacher
3. **Picasso was born in:**
   a. France
   b. England
   c. Spain ✓
4. **What does twisted mean?**
   a. dark
   b. crooked ✓
   c. cold
5. **Most artists probably:**
   a. do not always draw like Picasso ✓
   b. do not draw pictures
   c. do not paint

Page 62

Name _____ Date _____

Wilt the Stilt

Wilt **Chamberlain** is over seven feet tall. But he also stands tall as a fine basketball player. He set some records that have never been broken. During the 1961-62 season, he made more than 4,000 points. In one game he scored 100 points.

He was always a great player but people used to call him a loser. Even though he made a lot of points every game, his teams used to lose. People said he didn't care about his teams, but he did. In 1967, he proved that he could be a good team player too. Wilt was playing with the **Philadelphia** 76ers. He helped them win the championship. He didn't make a lot of points himself. But he helped keep the ball away from the other team.

In 1970 he joined the Los Angeles Lakers. He helped them win the championship in 1972. Wilt Chamberlain was voted best player of the year three times in a row.

1. **The main idea of this story is:**
   a. Wilt Chamberlain is very tall.
   b. Wilt didn't want to play for the Philadelphia 76ers.
   c. Wilt was a great basketball player. ✓
2. **Chamberlain was called "Wilt the Stilt" because:**
   a. He stood on stilts.
   b. He was always jumping up and down.
   c. He was very tall. ✓
3. **What was the most points Wilt scored during one game?**
   a. 250
   b. 100 ✓
   c. 75
4. **What does scored mean?**
   a. made points ✓
   b. bought food
   c. hit the ball
5. **Wilt was voted best player of the year because:**
   a. He was the tallest man on his team.
   b. He helped his team win. ✓
   c. He ran very fast.

Page 63

Name _____ Date _____

Woman of Two Worlds

Maria Tallchief is an **Osage** Indian. Her father was a chief, but her family did not practice the Indian ways. However, her grandmother Elizabeth Bigheart told Maria many stories about their tribe.

Maria began taking dance lessons when she was four years old. She practiced very hard and became a good dancer. She learned to jump high in the air and dance on her toes. When she was eighteen she joined a ballet company. She was asked to change her name because it did not sound like a dancer's name. But Maria was very proud to be an Indian and kept her name.

Soon she became very famous. A dance was made just for her. It was called "The Firebird". Maria played a beautiful bird with magic powers. Everyone thought Maria was wonderful in the part.

The Osage people made Maria a princess and called her "The Woman of Two Worlds". Although Maria lived far from her people, she always remembered them.

1. **The main idea of this story is:**
   a. Maria Tallchief played the piano.
   b. Maria Tallchief was a firebird.
   c. Maria Tallchief was a great dancer. ✓
2. **Ballet dancers dance:**
   a. on their toes ✓
   b. in the water
   c. on table tops
3. **What was the name of Maria's tribe?**
   a. Two Worlds
   b. Bigheart
   c. Osage ✓
4. **What does remember mean?**
   a. to forget about
   b. to go to
   c. to think of ✓
5. **Maria probably became a good dancer because:**
   a. She played the bongo drums.
   b. She practiced every day. ✓
   c. She owned a dancing school.

Page 64

120

Answer Key

Get a Horse

People laughed at the first cars. They ran on steam and were very noisy. They spilled smoke and hot coals into the air. Then the electric car was developed in 1890. It was quiet and did not dirty the air. But it could not travel more than 20 miles per hour. Also, the car's batteries had to be charged every 50 miles.

Gradually, the gasoline-powered car became the most popular. Henry Ford developed one of these cars. It had a single seat, bicycle wheels and an electric bell.

The early cars were very expensive. But Henry Ford believed that everyone should have a car. His factory began to make cars more quickly and at less cost. His most popular car was the Model T. It only cost $400.

Henry Ford developed the V-8 engine. It is a very strong engine that is still used in cars today. Henry spent the last part of his life working to help other people.

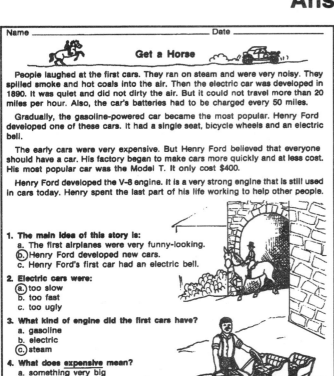

1. The main idea of this story is:
   a. The first airplanes were very funny-looking.
   (b.) Henry Ford developed new cars.
   c. Henry Ford's first car had an electric bell.

2. Electric cars were:
   (a.) too slow
   b. too fast
   c. too ugly

3. What kind of engine did the first cars have?
   a. gasoline
   b. electric
   (c.) steam

4. What does expensive mean?
   a. something very big
   (b.) something that costs a lot of money
   c. something very cold to eat

5. If people still drove electric cars:
   a. We would run out of water.
   b. The air would be very dirty.
   (c.) It would take longer to get places.

Page 65

A World Without Sun

Jacques **Cousteau** sails around the world on his ship **Calypso**. He films the underwater world. He has shown seals playing in the water and seagulls hunting for their dinner. He has filmed walruses floating on icebergs in the Arctic. Jacques has also shown sharks sleeping in caves in Mexico. On one trip he even found a Greek ship that had been buried under the sea for over 2,000 years.

Jacques Cousteau believes that someday man will live under the oceans. In 1963 he tried to prove that was possible. He and four divers lived in an underwater house for one month. The house was filled with air so the men could breathe.

Jacques Cousteau loves the ocean and all its living things. He gets very angry when people dump oil and garbage in it. He does everything he can do to protect it. Once he stopped France from dumping dangerous materials in the ocean.

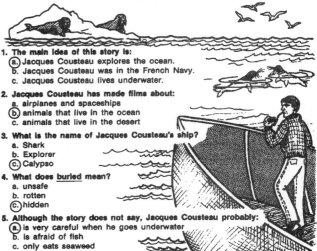

1. The main idea of this story is:
   (a.) Jacques Cousteau explores the ocean.
   b. Jacques Cousteau was in the French Navy.
   c. Jacques Cousteau lives underwater.

2. Jacques Cousteau has made films about:
   a. airplanes and spaceships
   (b.) animals that live in the ocean
   c. animals that live in the desert

3. What is the name of Jacques Cousteau's ship?
   a. Shark
   b. Explorer
   (c.) Calypso

4. What does buried mean?
   a. unsafe
   b. rotten
   (c.) hidden

5. Although the story does not say, Jacques Cousteau probably:
   (a.) is very careful when he goes underwater
   b. is afraid of fish
   c. only eats seaweed

Page 66

He Searched for His Past

When Alex Haley was a boy, his grandmother used to tell him stories about their family. She told Alex about his long-dead ancestor, **Kunta Kinte**. Kunta Kinte had come to America on a slave ship. Alex Haley decided that one day he would write the story of his family.

Many years later Alex Haley decided he was ready to write about his family. He spent twelve years studying his family history. He went to Africa and searched for his relatives. He found the Kinte family.

Alex Haley's book was called Roots. It told how Kunta Kinte tried to escape to freedom. He also wrote about Kunta's daughter, Kizzy, who was one of the few slaves who could read and write. Alex wrote stories about his other ancestors all the way down to his father. Alex wrote stories about himself, too.

Roots was made into a television motion picture. It was one of the most popular movies in television history.

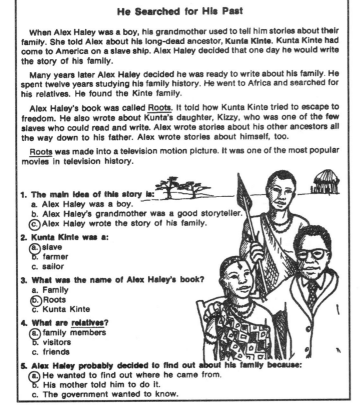

1. The main idea of this story is:
   a. Alex Haley was a boy.
   b. Alex Haley's grandmother was a good storyteller.
   (c.) Alex Haley wrote the story of his family.

2. Kunta Kinte was a:
   (a.) slave
   b. farmer
   c. sailor

3. What was the name of Alex Haley's book?
   a. Family
   (b.) Roots
   c. Kunta Kinte

4. What are relatives?
   (a.) family members
   b. visitors
   c. friends

5. Alex Haley probably decided to find out about his family because:
   (a.) He wanted to find out where he came from.
   b. His mother told him to do it.
   c. The government wanted to know.

Page 67

A Real Winner

Billie Jean King began playing tennis after school when she was eleven. She decided then that she was going to be a winner. She worked very hard. Soon she became one of America's best young tennis players.

Billie Jean King began to play in important tennis matches and she usually won. She won first place at the United States Open three times. She also won first place at the **Wimbledon** Matches in England six times.

In 1973, she faced one of the most important tennis matches of her life. Tennis player Bobby Riggs said women's tennis was just a big joke. He said he could beat the best woman tennis player. And Billie Jean was the best. She agreed to play against him.

On September 20, 1973, Billie Jean King met Bobby Riggs in the **Astrodome in Houston, Texas**. People all over the United States watched the game on television. The Astrodome was crowded with people. When Billie Jean won, the crowd cheered and cheered.

1. The main idea of this story is:
   a. Billie Jean King likes to tell jokes.
   (b.) Billie Jean King was a great tennis player.
   c. Bobby Riggs likes to knit.

2. Bobby Riggs thought:
   (a.) Women weren't as good tennis players as men.
   b. He was the best football player in the world.
   c. He could swim faster than any woman.

3. The Astrodome is in:
   a. Paris
   (b.) Houston
   c. New York

4. The word crowded means:
   a. empty
   (b.) full
   c. wet

5. Billie Jean King believed that:
   (a.) Women's tennis was important.
   b. Bobby Riggs should go back to school.
   c. Tennis was a silly game.

Page 68

FS-32046 Reading

Answer Key

Name _____ **Date** _____

Clowning Around

On the screen, the Marx Brothers moved like a whirlwind. Groucho chomped on his cigar and made jokes. Chico pretended to speak Italian. Harpo chased people around the room. They wore silly clothes and did crazy stunts. The sillier they acted, the more people laughed.

In one movie, the Marx Brothers decided to take a boat trip. They got a very tiny cabin which was soon filled with people and luggage. Soon there was no room, but people kept coming in. Finally, someone opened the cabin door and everyone tumbled out onto the floor.

The Marx Brothers really were brothers. They began performing when they were still children. Their other brothers, Zeppo and Gummo, also appeared with them for awhile.

Some of the Marx Brothers films are "Animal Crackers", "Duck Soup" and "A Night at the Opera". All of their films were made in the 1930's and 1940's. But children and adults still enjoy the Marx Brothers films today.

1. The main idea of this story is:
   a. The Marx Brothers took a trip.
   (b.) The Marx Brothers made people laugh.
   c. The Marx Brothers spoke Italian.

2. The Marx Brothers:
   (a.) made movies a long time ago
   b. were singing stars
   c. only made sad movies

3. How many Marx Brothers were there?
   a. 2
   b. 8
   (c.) 5

4. What does chomped mean?
   (a.) chewed
   b. swallowed
   c. jumped

5. People thought the Marx Brothers were very funny because:
   (a.) They wore funny clothes and acted silly.
   b. They were brothers.
   c. They never worked alone.

Page 69

Name _____ **Date** _____

The "Say Hey" Kid

Willie Mays was born to play baseball. His first toy was a baseball. He was given his first baseball glove when he was three years old. His father, grandfather, and uncle had all been baseball players. They began teaching Willie to play baseball when he was only six years old.

Willie joined the New York Giants when he was 20. He was good at everything he did in baseball. He was a great hitter. He won the batting championship in 1954. He also stole more than 300 bases. Willie could catch almost any ball that was hit into the outfield. Some of the catches he made seemed impossible to do.

Willie Mays was loved by sports fans. They called him the "Say Hey" kid because he could never remember anyone's name. He called everyone "Say Hey".

In 1973, Willie Mays left baseball at the age of 42. He had hit 660 home runs and had played almost 3,000 games.

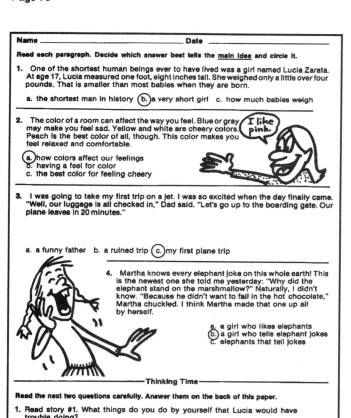

1. The main idea of this story is:
   (a.) Willie Mays was a champion baseball player.
   b. Willie Mays liked to play football.
   c. Willie Mays lived in New York.

2. The New York Giants:
   a. were very tall
   b. ate too much
   (c.) are a baseball team

3. To steal bases means:
   a. carry the bases away
   (b.) run the bases before the next batter up gets a hit
   c. hide under the base

4. Willie was called the "Say Hey" kid because:
   a. He liked to talk a lot.
   b. He liked to eat hay.
   (c.) He could never remember anyone's name.

5. Willie Mays probably left baseball because:
   a. He didn't like baseball anymore.
   b. He wanted to be a teacher.
   (c.) He was getting too old to play well.

Page 70

Name _____ **Date** _____

Read each paragraph. Decide which answer best tells the main idea and circle it.

1. The Komodo Dragon is actually a lizard. It can grow to be 10 feet long and is the largest lizard living today. The Komodo is called a dragon because it looks like one—long tail, sharp teeth and scaly skin.

   a. how long dragons grow   b. another name for lizards   (c.) what Komodos look like

2. A phobia is something you are afraid of. You might have a fear of cats or spiders or a fear of being in crowds. But here is a phobia to end all phobias: arachibutyrophobia! It is the fear of getting peanut butter stuck in the roof of your mouth.

   a. where peanut butter sticks
   (b.) fears called phobias
   c. a phobia about cats

3. Do you have a lot of insects wandering around the house? If so, a toad would make a great pet. Toads eat only foods that move—bugs, flies, beetles and other pests. Toads get very hungry in the summer. It takes 10,000 insects to fill up their stomachs. So don't swat any flies! Your toad might croak!

   a. how many flies toads eat   b. what toads like to eat   (c.) a good house pet

4. Once there was a man named John. He lived in England in a town called Sandwich. John loved to play cards. He never wanted to leave the card table, not even for meals. One day, John came up with a brilliant idea: "Why not just put some meat between two pieces of bread? Then I can play cards and eat at the same time." Today John's invention is known as the sandwich.

   (a.) a brilliant invention
   b. the man who invented bread
   c. eating at a card table

— Thinking Time —

Read the next two questions carefully. Answer them on the back of this paper.

1. People are terribly afraid of many different things. How do you think someone might have developed a fear of water?

2. Finish this sentence in your own words: John eats a sandwich and plays cards at the same time. I eat a sandwich and _____.

Page 71

Name _____ **Date** _____

Read each paragraph. Decide which answer best tells the main idea and circle it.

1. One of the shortest human beings ever to have lived was a girl named Lucia Zarata. At age 17, Lucia measured one foot, eight inches tall. She weighed only a little over four pounds. That is smaller than most babies when they are born.

   a. the shortest man in history   (b.) a very short girl   c. how much babies weigh

2. The color of a room can affect the way you feel. Blue or gray may make you feel sad. Yellow and white are cheery colors. Peach is the best color of all, though. This color makes you feel relaxed and comfortable.

   (a.) how colors affect our feelings
   b. having a feel for color
   c. the best color for feeling cheery

3. I was going to take my first trip on a jet. I was so excited when the day finally came. "Well, our luggage is all checked in," Dad said. "Let's go up to the boarding gate. Our plane leaves in 20 minutes."

   a. a funny father   b. a ruined trip   (c.) my first plane trip

4. Martha knows every elephant joke on this whole earth! This is the newest one she told me yesterday: "Why did the elephant stand on the marshmallow?" Naturally, I didn't know. "Because he didn't want to fall in the hot chocolate," Martha chuckled. I think Martha made that one up all by herself.

   a. a girl who likes elephants
   (b.) a girl who tells elephant jokes
   c. elephants that tell jokes

— Thinking Time —

Read the next two questions carefully. Answer them on the back of this paper.

1. Read story #1. What things do you do by yourself that Lucia would have trouble doing?

2. Tell how each of these colors might make you feel: red, purple, black, brown, and orange.

Page 72

122

Answer Key

Name _____ Date _____

Read each paragraph. Decide which answer best tells the <u>main idea</u> and circle it.

1. Once a man lost the tip of his nose in a fight. He had a new tip made out of gold. The man polished his nose all the time. It really shined! He was very proud of it. He did have trouble blowing his gold nose, though.

   a. having a fight   b. how to make a gold nose   (c.) a new nose

2. Why wasn't the New World named after Christopher Columbus? Until the day he died, Columbus insisted that he had discovered an unexplored area of Asia. If Columbus had known his geography better, we might be called Columbians and not Americans today.

   (a.) the naming of the New World
   b. who really discovered America
   c. exploring land in Asia

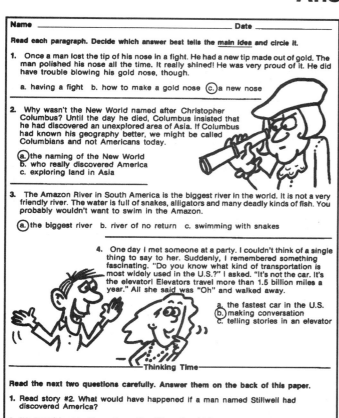

3. The Amazon River in South America is the biggest river in the world. It is not a very friendly river. The water is full of snakes, alligators and many deadly kinds of fish. You probably wouldn't want to swim in the Amazon.

   (a.) the biggest river   b. river of no return   c. swimming with snakes

4. One day I met someone at a party. I couldn't think of a single thing to say to her. Suddenly, I remembered something fascinating. "Do you know what kind of transportation is most widely used in the U.S.?" I asked. "It's not the car. It's the elevator! Elevators travel more than 1.5 billion miles a year." All she said was "Oh" and walked away.

   a. the fastest car in the U.S.
   (b.) making conversation
   c. telling stories in an elevator

—Thinking Time—

Read the next two questions carefully. Answer them on the back of this paper.

1. Read story #2. What would have happened if a man named Stillwell had discovered America?

2. We travel by car. Name four other things in which you can travel.

Page 73

Name _____ Date _____

Read each paragraph. Decide which answer best tells the <u>main idea</u> and circle it.

1. This is something that will bring you good luck: put a corn cob behind your ear. Be sure to eat the corn first, though.

   a. wishing for corn   (b.) a good luck charm   c. how corn grows

2. The cheetah is the fastest land animal on earth. This cat can sprint up to 70 miles an hour! Imagine a cheetah running alongside your car while you are driving down the highway! Both of you would get a ticket for going over the speed limit.

   a. running 70 miles per hour
   (b.) the fastest animal
   c. speeding on the highway

3. Once there were two painters, Gus and Georgy, working on a house. Georgy was on the ladder and Gus was mixing paints below. "Have you got a tight grip on that paint brush?" Gus called up to Georgy.
   Georgy answered, "Yes sire-e-e."
   "Good!" Gus said. "Hang on 'cause I need the ladder." Gus took the ladder away.

   a. painting a house   b. using a paint brush   (c.) a surprised painter

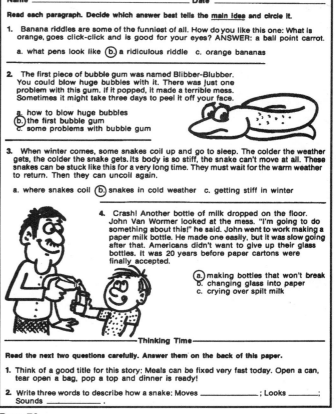

4. Long ago, people lit their Christmas trees by fastening real candles on the branches. Many trees with these decorations burned down. Then someone suggested using electric lights instead. These white lights were not very popular at first. But when they were painted red, blue and green, everyone started using electric lights on their trees.

   a. lighting up Christmas trees
   b. why candles are dangerous
   (c.) how electric lights first became popular

—Thinking Time—

Read the next two questions carefully. Answer them on the back of this paper.

1. Corn is supposed to bring good luck. Name two other kinds of good luck charms you know about.

2. Read story #3. Draw a picture to show the expression on Georgy's face when Gus took the ladder.

Page 74

Name _____ Date _____

Read each paragraph. Decide which answer best tells the <u>main idea</u> and circle it.

1. Not long ago, there lived a man who never slept a day in his life. Doctors watched him day and night for months. He never took so much as a cat nap! Only once did this man sleep—on the day he died at age 94!

   a. sleeping for 94 years   b. how to live without sleep   (c.) a man who never slept

2. Thousands of years ago, people had only one name—Gregory, for example. When someone talked about Gregory, they would say, "Gregory of Albans is coming to see me." This was very simple—until too many Gregorys were born in Albans. Read the next story to find out what happened.

   a. where Gregorys are born
   b. how people were named
   (c.) how many names people had

3. Your last name is your **surname**. Let's say your name is Anthony. Your father's name is John. Your full name would be Anthony Johnson (son-of-John). This was just one of many ways used to make surnames. Today, everyone has at least two names. Some people have seven or eight names.

   (a.) how surnames are made   b. what Johnson means   c. when surnames are used

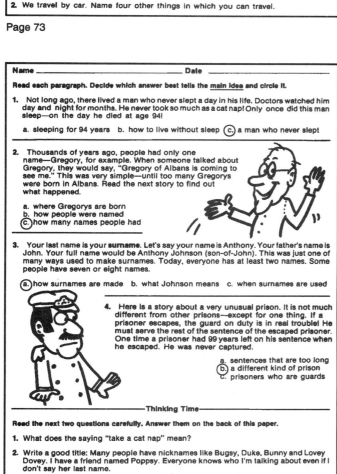

4. Here is a story about a very unusual prison. It is not much different from other prisons—except for one thing. If a prisoner escapes, the guard on duty is in real trouble! He must serve the rest of the sentence of the escaped prisoner. One time a prisoner had 99 years left on his sentence when he escaped. He was never captured.

   a. sentences that are too long
   (b.) a different kind of prison
   c. prisoners who are guards

—Thinking Time—

Read the next two questions carefully. Answer them on the back of this paper.

1. What does the saying "take a cat nap" mean?

2. Write a good title: Many people have nicknames like Bugsy, Duke, Bunny and Lovey Dovey. I have a friend named Poppsy. Everyone knows who I'm talking about even if I don't say her last name.

Page 75

Name _____ Date _____

Read each paragraph. Decide which answer best tells the <u>main idea</u> and circle it.

1. Banana riddles are some of the funniest of all. How do you like this one: What is orange, goes click-click and is good for your eyes? ANSWER: a ball point carrot.

   a. what pens look like   (b.) a ridiculous riddle   c. orange bananas

2. The first piece of bubble gum was named Blibber-Blubber. You could blow huge bubbles with it. There was just one problem with this gum. If it popped, it made a terrible mess. Sometimes it might take three days to peel it off your face.

   a. how to blow huge bubbles
   (b.) the first bubble gum
   c. some problems with bubble gum

3. When winter comes, some snakes coil up and go to sleep. The colder the weather gets, the colder the snake gets. Its body is so stiff, the snake can't move at all. These snakes can be stuck like this for a very long time. They must wait for the warm weather to return. Then they can uncoil again.

   a. where snakes coil   (b.) snakes in cold weather   c. getting stiff in winter

4. Crash! Another bottle of milk dropped on the floor. John Van Wormer looked at the mess. "I'm going to do something about this!" he said. John went to work making a paper milk bottle. He made one easily, but it was slow going after that. Americans didn't want to give up their glass bottles. It was 20 years before paper cartons were finally accepted.

   (a.) making bottles that won't break
   b. changing glass into paper
   c. crying over spilt milk

—Thinking Time—

Read the next two questions carefully. Answer them on the back of this paper.

1. Think of a good title for this story: Meals can be fixed very fast today. Open a can, tear open a bag, pop a top and dinner is ready!

2. Write three words to describe how a snake: Moves _____ ; Looks _____ Sounds _____ .

Page 76

FS-32046 Reading

Answer Key

Name _____ **Date** _____

Read each paragraph. Decide which answer best tells the main idea and circle it.

1. In the early 1800's, schools were called "blab schools". That's because everyone blabbed! The whole class said their lessons out loud—all at the same time.

   (a.) what schools were called   b. lessons in blabbing   c. blabbing out loud

2. Dip. Write. Dip. Write. Into the ink bottle, back to the paper. Writing with a fountain pen took a long time. It could be very messy, too. And at school, boys liked to dip girls' pigtails into the ink bottles. Why couldn't there be a pen with the ink already in it? Someone did finally invent the ball point pen. Now everyone just "clicks and writes". Today, fountain pens are mainly a decoration on a desk.

   a. the end of ink bottles
   (b.) a new way to write with ink
   c. where fountain pens are found

3. The largest bird in the world is the ostrich. It is eight feet tall and weighs more than 300 pounds. The ostrich can't fly, but it really doesn't need to. At full speed it can run 50 miles an hour.

   a. an unusual bird   (b.) world's largest bird   c. why ostriches can't fly

4. Can you imagine never missing a day of school for twelve years? One student accomplished this by getting sick only on weekends and holidays. Another one kept four alarm clocks in his room. And there was the girl who went to school in a one-room schoolhouse. It was her school during the day and her home at night. School was held even when she was sick. She just sat in bed and listened to the lessons.

   (a.) perfect attendance
   b. twelve years in school
   c. attending at home

— Thinking Time —

Read the next two questions carefully. Answer them on the back of this paper.

1. The potato chip and french fries were invented by a cook 100 years ago. How do you think they came to be invented?

2. If you have "set a record" what have you done?

Page 77

Name _____ **Date** _____

Read each paragraph. Decide which answer best tells the main idea and circle it.

1. As we get older, our sense of smell gets old, too. The nose seems to give out faster than any of the other sense organs. That's probably a good thing, especially if you live near a garbage dump.

   a. the smell of garbage   (b.) when noses get old   c. sensing a smell

2. Do you have a sore throat? Get a piece of raw meat and put some pepper on it. Wrap it around your neck for a few days. This is what people did 100 years ago. When the meat turned rotten, the sore throat got better (or you got even sicker from the smell).

   a. how meat makes you sick
   b. why throats are sore
   (c.) a cure for sore throats

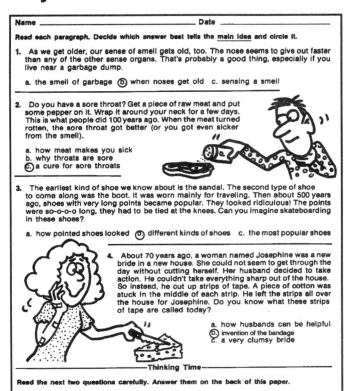

3. The earliest kind of shoe we know about is the sandal. The second type of shoe to come along was the boot. It was worn mainly for traveling. Then about 500 years ago, shoes with very long points became popular. They looked ridiculous! The points were so-o-o-o long, they had to be tied at the knees. Can you imagine skateboarding in these shoes?

   a. how pointed shoes looked   (b.) different kinds of shoes   c. the most popular shoes

4. About 70 years ago, a woman named Josephine was a new bride in a new house. She could not seem to get through the day without cutting herself. Her husband decided to take action. He couldn't take everything sharp out of the house. So instead, he cut up strips of tape. A piece of cotton was stuck in the middle of each strip. He left the strips all over the house for Josephine. Do you know what these strips of tape are called today?

   a. how husbands can be helpful
   (b.) invention of the bandage
   c. a very clumsy bride

— Thinking Time —

Read the next two questions carefully. Answer them on the back of this paper.

1. Think of a good title for this story: Your mouth can make sounds, hum a tune, play the trumpet and blow bubbles.

2. Name five different activities for which you need to buy five different kinds of shoes.

Page 78

Name _____ **Date** _____

Read each paragraph. Decide which answer best tells the main idea and circle it.

1. There are some green sheep wandering around England. They have lawns growing on their backs! How could this be? Someone must have dropped grass seeds onto their wool. With all the sun and rain, the seeds grew. The sheep don't seem to mind. But what if someone decides to mow the lawn?

   a. growing grass seeds   (b.) greenback sheep   c. little grass sheep

2. Long ago, people guessed what time it was by looking at the sun. Later "shadow sticks" were set in the ground. When the shadow was the shortest, it was noontime. From the shadow stick came the sundial. It is one of the oldest known instruments for telling time. Other early time-telling instruments were the hourglass and the water clock.

   a. how shadow sticks tell time
   (b.) early ways to tell time
   c. telling time by the sun

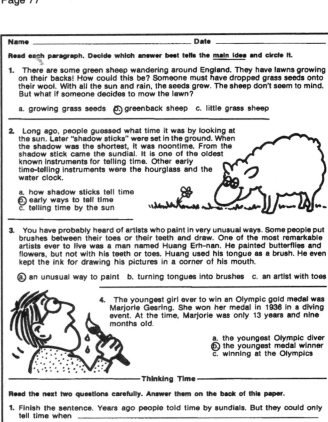

3. You have probably heard of artists who paint in very unusual ways. Some people put brushes between their toes or their teeth and draw. One of the most remarkable artists ever to live was a man named Huang Erh-nan. He painted butterflies and flowers, but not with his teeth or toes. Huang used his tongue as a brush. He even kept the ink for drawing his pictures in a corner of his mouth.

   (a.) an unusual way to paint   b. turning tongues into brushes   c. an artist with toes

4. The youngest girl ever to win an Olympic gold medal was Marjorie Gesring. She won her medal in 1936 in a diving event. At the time, Marjorie was only 13 years and nine months old.

   a. the youngest Olympic diver
   (b.) the youngest medal winner
   c. winning at the Olympics

— Thinking Time —

Read the next two questions carefully. Answer them on the back of this paper.

1. Finish the sentence. Years ago people told time by sundials. But they could only tell time when _____

2. Ben is a champion skateboarder. He has won many contest. He would like to be in the Olympics. Why can't he?

Page 79

Name _____ **Date** _____

Read each paragraph. Decide which answer best tells the main idea and circle it.

1. There are a lot of different sayings about noses: The horse won by a nose. She's got a nose for news. He hit it right on the nose! Do you know what these sayings mean?

   a. how horses win races   b. learning sayings   (c.) sayings about noses

2. A tree in California known as "General Sherman" is one of the oldest living things in the world. This giant sequoia is 272 feet tall and still growing. Scientists think the tree was "born" at least 3,000 to 4,000 years ago. That's really living to a ripe old age.

   a. the oldest living person in the world
   b. who General Sherman was
   (c.) the oldest living sequoia

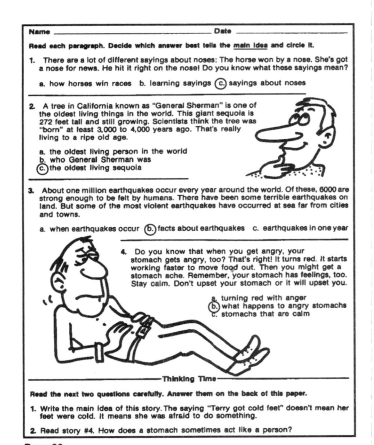

3. About one million earthquakes occur every year around the world. Of these, 6000 are strong enough to be felt by humans. There have been some terrible earthquakes on land. But some of the most violent earthquakes have occurred at sea far from cities and towns.

   a. when earthquakes occur   (b.) facts about earthquakes   c. earthquakes in one year

4. Do you know that when you get angry, your stomach gets angry, too? That's right! It turns red. It starts working faster to move food out. Then you might get a stomach ache. Remember, your stomach has feelings, too. Stay calm. Don't upset your stomach or it will upset you.

   a. turning red with anger
   (b.) what happens to angry stomachs
   c. stomachs that are calm

— Thinking Time —

Read the next two questions carefully. Answer them on the back of this paper.

1. Write the main idea of this story. The saying "Terry got cold feet" doesn't mean her feet were cold. It means she was afraid to do something.

2. Read story #4. How does a stomach sometimes act like a person?

Page 80

FS-32046 Reading